iii

Contents

D1578732

Caring for people: Making the change

SIR WILLIAM UTTING

It is a shock to recall that seven years have passed since the White Paper *Caring for People* was published in November 1989. This is the clearest and fullest exposition we have – or are likely to have – of the policy of community care and the values that inform it . Everybody working in community care ought to carry with them, as a personal mission statement, a summary of the broad objectives of that policy: enabling people to live normal lives in their own homes, helping people to achieve independence and their full potential, and giving them a greater say in how they live their lives and in the services they need.

The further in time we are from *Caring for People* the greater becomes the need to remind ourselves of the broad values and key components of the policy and the objectives which government set itself. They are already in danger of being obscured by the host of secondary, organisational goals which have been set up: the re-structuring of departments, the separation of purchaser from provider, the procedures for assessment and contracting – a concentration on process almost as an end in itself. *Caring for People* is inspired by some of the basic values of social work. Social workers ought therefore to be particularly vigilant in protecting and promulgating the values and objectives of community care.

I have said many times that training is the greatest challenge of community care. Its success depends upon managers and other staff re-orienting both attitudes and practice. Social workers, no less than other staff, must re-examine the way they view the people they work with and the methods they use. I am in no doubt that the need for 'traditional' social work, like the need for other community services, will continue to increase. Social workers must be prepared to act as advocates of their own specialism in making sure that the need for it is not squeezed out by the demand for more obvious material services.

But social workers – and social work educators – must also be prepared to adapt to changing times. Social work demands of its practioners that they remain sensitive to changing social need and adjust their practice to meet it. The American-influenced social casework on which I cut my professional teeth has been supplemented and supplanted by group work, community work, 'generic' work, task-centred casework, patch work and community social work – to name perhaps only a few. It is now time for some social workers to extend their range to care management, for which they are in my view particularly well qualified because of their skills in assessment and in coordinating inter-service activity. Social workers will in future need grounding in care management and contracting as well as in the basics of their craft. That is the challenge for them, and for their educators.

Introduction

STEVE TREVILLION and PETER BERESFORD

When the history of social work in the twentieth century comes to be written, the years 1968 and 1988 will surely figure prominently: 1968 was the year of the Seebohm Report which ushered in the era of generic social work; 1988 was the year of the Griffiths Report which together with the 1990 National Health Service and Community Care Act ushered in the present era. It is still too early to write this history. We are still living it. But one thing is certain. During the 1990s social work changed and continues to change. It has changed profoundly, probably irrevocably and in large part because of community care. Generic social work is dead and with it lies the dream of a social casework solution to social problems. Something else is taking its place. What that something is, we cannot yet know, but we can be sure that it is emerging in the context of the often painful encounter with community care and in particular the encounter with three potentially revolutionary ideas: involvement of service uses, the mixed economy of care and collaboration. It is this encounter and in particular its implications for social work education and training which is the subject of this book.

The book aims to focus attention on a two-part question. Does the disappearance of generic Seebohm-style social work mean that in the aftermath of the community care reforms we need a revolution in social work education and training comparable to the revolution rolling through every field of social work practice? If so, what kind of revolution is it that is needed?

We have been surprised at how few and far between have been the attempts to find answers to this question, despite its increasing importance. The move away from traditional notions of professional education to what are frequently referred to as 'competency driven' models of training, has generated a heated debate in the social work press. But where is the debate about the curriculum? One might have expected the recent review of social work education and training to break the silence, but at best it has generated only a muted conversation. This is our attempt to stimulate the kind of creative thinking about complex ethical, political, economic and psychological issues which has always been one of the best features of the social work tradition and to focus this on community care, not as a policy or even a set of tasks but rather as a crucible for the transformation of professional roles and identities.

This book is built around three key questions. What are the implications for social work of:

- the development of user-led services?

- the mixed economy of care?

- the new emphasis on collaborative and interprofessional forms of work?

These questions provide the framework for the book and for the spitit of inquiry and open-ended discussion which the contributors bring to it.

This book draws in many different perspectives, including service users, managers, policy makers, academics, trainers, educators and researchers. They bring to the discussion different histories, experience, cultures, expectations and philosophies. This is reflected in the different styles in which they write, as well as their different approaches to the subject. Some contributors wear more than one hat. Readers will encounter different concepts, ideologies and language. They will, for example, see people referred to variously as clients, service users and survivors, reflecting all the different beliefs and values that go with each of these terms. Readers can expect to read impassioned argument as well as closely argued analysis. Some contributions include references, others do not. We have deliberately sought not to homogenise or standardise the different contributions, but instead to allow them to speak for themselves. We have done this to reflect the breadth and diversity of current discussion about community care. It is no longer the narrow concern of politicians, policy makers and professionals. This is another of the challenges that face educators.

There is no consensus here. Edited collections like this usually bring together like-minded people to cast their complementary light on a subject. But the key themes which together make up the community care revolution do not encourage this approach. They do not necessarily sit comfortably together.

Developments like user-led services and the mixed economy of care are as likely to be antagonistic as complementary. We certainly did not want to impose an artificial consensus on contributors. They reflect the diversity of views and values inherent in community care itself. What some see as gains, others see as problems. We suspect that each reader will find some things which they don't agree with in the book, as well as many with which they do. This is certainly the case for us. Not only is community care a contentious subject, but it has also made it possible for most if not all stakeholders to add their voice to the debate – something rare in welfare.

What we also hope is that conflicts and contradictions which emerge in this book will offer readers the opportunity to form their own judgements and come to their own conclusions. Social work educators will need to be familiar with the tensions and disagreements which the book highlights and demarcates. Social work education is also throwing up its own parallel and related set of conflicts (*Community Care*, 1995). The community care revolution has generated new theories, new roles, new balances of power and new relationships. We hope that this book will be helpful to readers both by acquainting them with these and helping them find their way through them.

The book is based on a national conference organised jointly by Brunel University College and the National Institute for Social Work and supported by the Central Council for Education and Training in Social Work. As far as we know it is still the only discussion about social work education and the community care reforms which brings together the perspectives of service users, professionals and educators.

The book is divided into six sections. Daphne Statham sets the scene for the rest of the book in her wide ranging review of the 'challenges to social work education'. She locates these challenges within the context of the new 'globalism' of welfare services, characterised by rapid change and the creation of radically different kinds of network based organisations. She also reminds social workers and social work educators that not everyone within this new world is committed to the value of social work and that it is up to social work to make a case for itself rather than assuming that this is obvious to politicians and others.

She then identifies some of the specific challenges facing social work educators as they seek to prepare students for practice in a post welfare state world. These are: new stakeholders, increasing specialisation, participation and empowerment, work-based rather than college-based learning, the need to recognise that there are limits to what can be included in a crowded curriculum. She finally concludes with a plea to raise the status of practice.

Having sketched in the 'big picture' we then explore the first of our key themes: the challenge of educating and training for user-led services.

Peter Beresford highlights the centrality of service user involvement in the fundamental changes now taking place in social work specifically and social welfare generally. He points to the ways in which this involvement needs to be reflected in social work education if it is to meet the challenge of the community care revolution. New times demand new skills, new relationships and new understandings in social work practice. He argues that the development of user involvement in the provision, process and curriculum of social work education and training makes it possible to empower and equip practitioners to work effectively in the new user-led culture of community care.

Kath Gillespie Sells focuses on two key issues for social work educators raised by the community care reforms: equity and advocacy. She argues that involving service users fully as user trainers and consultants offers educators a way of addressing both successfully and of combatting discrimination.

Jan Wallcraft then develops this theme further in the next section, suggesting that social workers need to become the allies of service users and user groups, while in her contribution Miriam Hastings focuses on the implications of the demise of many paternalistic assumptions and the need to open up Approved Social Work training to involvement by user trainers. Whilst no easy answers are offered the nature of the challenge is identified very clearly. In case anyone should be tempted to look nostalgically back to the 'good old days' of Seebohm, Jan Wallcraft argues that the community care reforms represent an opportunity for social work education finally to enable social workers to be realistic about what they can and cannot do.

The fourth section explores the challenge of the care market to traditional professional assumptions. In his provocative piece on the subject of quasi-markets, Julian Le Grand claims that not only are quasi-markets transforming British public services, they are effectively transforming professional social work as well. His most controversial point is that "social workers will have to be trained to act, not so much as advocates for their clients, but as needs assessors and rationing agents". He also suggests that there needs to be a shift in the 'training culture' away from an intrinsic hostility to markets towards a more 'balanced' view.

This brings to the fore a key tension within the value system of community care and forces us to ask to what extent a market-led model is compatible with a user-led model of community care. It also forces us to ask how it is that social work education and training can address these conflicts rather than pretending that they don't exist or choosing to focus only on what seems compatible with traditional practices.

Bob Anderson explores this dilemma from an ethical perspective. He picks up the theme of markets in social work but develops it in a personal way to explore his own experiences of contracting and purchasing. He argues for the need to produce social workers who can combine commercial skills with care. This will inevitably involve new forms of knowledge, for example about contract law and finance, and new skills, for example in negotiation. One key theme running throughout this discussion is the need to pay attention to ethics, so that the market place is a principled rather than an unprincipled one. He argues cogently that purchasing and provider power can be used to create a more principled environment for the delivery of community care services. This leads him to conclude by suggesting that "purchasing and contracting is probably the best thing that has happened to social work in my lifetime".

Although not everyone will agree with him, he is certainly right to emphasise the importance of acknowledging the reality of the marketplace and seeking to understand one's own role within it. But what would happen to the traditional curriculum?

The next section of the book looks at our final theme – collaboration. In her contribution Maria Duggan also challenges some sacred cows by suggesting that it may be much more appropriate to think of social work as a kind of a public health activity than as something defined according to the traditional precepts of social casework. She argues that it is largely through the challenge of primary care and community care that this new 'public health' discourse is being created and that as it develops its essentially collaborative nature is becoming clear. She not only makes a powerful case for social workers to get involved in these new collaborative 'public health' activities, but also suggests that there are far reaching implications for social work education, including a much stronger emphasis on joint training with nurses and doctors than has hitherto been seen as either possible or desirable.

The implications of collaboration for social work education are explored in a more detailed and specific way by Steve Trevillion who focuses on questions of skill development in relation to the central community care skill of networking. He looks at the way in which networking has developed within the matrix of contemporary concerns about partnership, empower-ment and community. In particular he focuses on the 'soft revolution' associated with the community care reforms and consisting of the new emphasis on skills in joining with and working with others in a wide range of different contexts. He sees this as a 'post modern' social work for a 'post welfare state' world. He goes on to describe aspects of the new knowledge base and the new skills which social workers will need in order to work in this way.

Although collaboration has always seemed like one of those things everyone could agree was a 'good idea', Maria Duggan's and Steve Trevillion's discussions indicate very clearly that educating and training for collaboration involves a radical challenge to traditional assumptions about professional roles and relationships. The irony is that far from being simply oil on the troubled waters of community care, collaboration is an idea which once taken seriously could prove to be as controversial as the mixed economy of care or user involvement. And a good thing too! Neither social work nor community care need meaningless rhetoric or bland diplomacy.

The final section of the book consists of a look at the 'way forward' by Denise Platt. Like Bill Utting she stresses the key values and objectives of community care and connects these to the emergence of a new 'culture'. To work within the new culture she suggests that social workers will need to learn how to undertake a wide range of relatively unfamiliar activities such as care management and commissioning as well as more familiar tasks such as assessment.

In surveying the nature of the changes set in train by the reforms, she revisits all three of the book's key themes and shows how they are linked with one another. Although the scale of the challenge is daunting, she takes a positive view about the contribution of social work.

This essential optimism, tempered by an awareness of the very real problems and difficulties facing us all, permeates the papers in this collection. Together they add up to a persuasive case for the value of social work in the 1990s and beyond. But perhaps even more important, they begin to show how all of us who are concerned with educating our future social workers might begin to respond to the fundamental nature of the challenges associated with the 'community care revolution'.

Challenges to social work education

DAPHNE STATHAM

Introduction

We live in a time of rapid change, giving rise to a whole range of issues impacting on the nature and position of social work in the United Kingdom, with consequent implications for social work education. A number of these issues affect a wide range of interests. Boundaries are shifting all the time, new alliances of interests are being made, and the shape of the traditional strongholds of social work – statutory organisations and the large voluntary agencies – is changing. People are talking about 'virtual organisations' – groupings of people from different agencies, from business, from banking, for example, coming together with parents and people with learning difficulties, to purchase independent accommodation and care packages.

These 'virtual organisations' are delivering what existing structures at present find difficult, or make the process so cumbersome, that the tendency is to find ways around the blocks. The options for achieving change are increasing. Moreover, the degree of control or separateness we will be able to maintain in working through the impact of such changes on social work is likely to continue to be less than we might wish. The general buffeting we are currently receiving will doubtless continue.

External challenges

The challenge to the role of the professional

Social work is not alone in facing challenges from politicians. We are part of a conscious central government plan to alter the balance of power between government itself, service users and carers, the public and the professions. It was not an oversight that social work was barely mentioned in the White Paper leading to the National Health Service and Community Care and Children Acts. We are simply not seen as one of the key stakeholders, but as one of the means through which the policies are implemented. The consequence is that not only is there a challenge about who does what – do we really need expensively trained social workers to undertake assessment and care management? – but also to the significance allocated to social work practice itself.

There is increasing emphasis on social care being everyone's responsibility, not just that of experts or specialists like ourselves. Social work is seen as one actor among many. There is a growing overlap between what care staff and carers need to know about and be able to do. Definitions of quality and good practice need to be negotiated between these different perspectives, not defined only by ourselves. It is now essential to think about including service users and carers in any staff development strategy if practice which promotes participation is to be achieved.

The changing role of central government in social work/social care

The traditional role of central government is to provide the legislative framework within which local government operates – but over the past decade central government's influence over the way local government does this work has been increasing. Eighty to eighty five per cent of local authority spending comes from central government grant – there is detailed guidance, centrally monitored, and powers of direction. "The effect is to move these services from being locally governed towards being locally administered according to central prescription and resourcing" (Harding, 1992).

The tension for social work is that part of the prescription is to provide individually tailored services in consultation with the people who use services – all of which requires a "high degree of local discretion and determination" and skilled staff. This can never be achieved by a form filling, procedural approach (Smale and Tuson, 1993). The way government policy has been formulated places social work and social care together with service users at the point of highest conflict between two opposing trends. The increasing interest in the content and outputs of social work training is a logical progression of the movement of welfare to the centre stage.

The withdrawal of central government from welfare

Throughout the European Union and more widely, there is a rethinking of the balance of responsibilities of the state, local communities and the family for the provision of social care. Even though most social care is provided through the family and in the main by women, all across the political spectrum there is concern about the cost of welfare. The evidence is that most expenditure is not on the personal social services but on social security benefits. Hill (1993) estimates that in 1992-93 just over one per cent of government spending on welfare as a whole in the United Kingdom went on the personal social services. This is less than its equivalent in most other countries in the European Union and is "the area where government probably plays the smallest role in total provision".

The primary means of coping with reduction of the resources provided through government is targeting – a move away from ensuring that underpinning resources are available to prevent individuals and families reaching crisis point, and hence falling into dependence on state provided resources. The accusation that social workers' values and methods pull people into long term dependence has to be put within this broader context. It also means that the priority given to particular skills and approaches is likely to change to an emphasis on those that promote independence and maximise existing social support systems. The sought-for position of the social worker with responsibility for assessing for and managing state resources will be "on the margins" (Smale, 1988) not in the centre of things as the expert.

Increasing numbers of people with an investment in social care

An increasing number of people have social care needs. Will Hutton (1995) writes of the three thirds society: that is one third either unemployed or living on benefits or low wages; another third insecure because of economic and technological change resulting in a culture where no one has a job for life anymore; while the final group are secure and insulated from understanding what is happening to the other two thirds. Put together with the increasing numbers of people who have responsibilities towards elderly people, the tradition of a minority with an investment in social care is changing.

Divorce and the increasing number of mothers who are in employment means that women's wages are central in keeping families out of poverty and dependence on benefits. Yet there is no adequate system of child care to enable them to work. An illustration of the size of the change is the National Society for the Prevention of Cruelty to Children's *Home Alone* leaflet advising parents and carers on what risks they cannot or should not take. Mothers in employment are not a new historical phenomenon, but the context in which this is taking place, and higher expectations of standards of child care means that social education is required to support parenting in this new scenario.

Increasing the responsibilities carried by families and local communities without the back up of underpinning resources may mean that more people are pushed into crisis and hence into dependence on scarce state provision. Social workers are not alone in talking about preventive services – employers also have an interest since increasing numbers of their employees have responsibilities for the care of children and dependent adults.

Nor is this seen anymore as solely a women's issue. The question of how the demands of work and family life are kept in balance and how to share responsibilities for resources is being debated among government departments and by business internationally. The Confederation of British Industry and the European Commision are talking about 'family friendly' employment policies.

A consequence of this new awareness is that we may be developing a concept of social care which is akin to that of public and environmental health. That is where the major health gains this century have been made. Protection of children is better achieved by thinking about what constitutes a safe environment for children, by taking into account the life and employment patterns of parents rather than by continuing to increase the number of child protection investigations.

The breakdown of the traditional division between work life and family life

The traditional division between the workplace and the family is breaking down. The Confederation of British Industry is concerned about what can be done to create an environment in which business can flourish, and have given support to the campaign for day nurseries as a means of developing and retaining a skilled workforce, in order to remain competitive as Asia and the Pacific Region develop industrially. At a Family Welfare

Association seminar on the future of welfare, Howard Davies was concerned about how to combat the tendency of some young people to lower their expectations to living on benefits, when the current nature of international markets means that Europe will flourish only if it has skilled labour to produce high quality goods (Family Welfare Association, 1994).

Holding on to skilled labour is crucial to business success. The Royal Society of Arts' inquiry into 'tomorrow's company' argues for a changed order of priorities for success in the international market: "The nature of competition is changing as the interdependence increases between companies and the community. In order to be internationally competitive the company requires a supportive operating environment". This interim report goes on to say that convential wisdom about promoting shareholders' interests as the prime purpose of business is now under challenge and argues for a more inclusive approach (RSA, 1994).

At a time when social services are increasingly being targeted on the few, there is a move towards looking at wider relevance for social care, as a means of social integration. In contrast to cost shifting – balancing the books of one agency by shifting the responsibility on to another – this approach looks at ways in which decisions about, for example, how money for adapting houses can impact on the underpinning support to promote independent living in the community, not long term dependence on state provided resources.

Similarly, decisions about providing accessible public transport have an impact not only on the mobility of disabled people but also on mothers with young children. Inter-disciplinary work is necessary not only to deliver direct services, but also to promote a supportive and inclusive environment. It is clear that the resources for this will not come from central government – whichever of our political parties is in power – but from shared responsibility among government, business, the voluntary sector and families. The role of volunteers, including those from industry and people in the third age, will inevitably take on greater significance in the provision of social care, as will the ability of social workers and care staff to work with and support them.

'Political correctness'

The European green paper on social policy emphasises the importance of social integration for groups excluded because of unemployment, disability, racism, poverty as essential for economic development in the Union (European Commission, 1994). It is ironic that preventive or open services to families are being reduced in many places. The voluntary sector, in particular small local groups including Black and minority ethnic and women's groups, is threatened in spite of evidence that Black and minority ethnic people receive more 'control' than 'support' services.

The challenge to 'political correctness', to social work's promotion of language which does not discriminate, cannot be seen in isolation from the general conflict that is taking place in this area. Whilst we in social work along with others are pioneering the debate, no public consensus has as yet been built up and this is still a contested area. This does not mean that we should give up what we have achieved, or cease to challenge accusations when they are built on assumption rather than fact, but that we have to chart the course of the political debate and think through our reactions to it.

However, there are also positive developments. The Acts require attention to race, religion and culture: the fact that Black and ethnic minority people are over-represented among homeless, poor, unemployed, imprisoned people, recipients of mental health services and those in care becomes a concern wider than that of social work if greater social cohesion is recognised as a condition for economic success. We are now joined by the police and the judges in acknowledging racism as a form of abuse, violence and injustice. Other good news is that, although patchy, there is evidence of some very good social work practice in promoting racial equality (Butt, 1994), and that more recently qualified social workers feel they have the skills to practice in a multi-ethnic society.

Implications for social work education

New stakeholders

All these challenges, on top of the mixed economy of care, mean that there are new stakeholders in social care. These changes will have an impact on the context in which professional skills are used, on which skills are valued, and on the place of social workers qualified to Diploma level. The employment base of social workers will become more diverse than in the past. Competence is likely to include the capacity to operate in, or at least understand enough about the different sectors to work with, if not within them. More students will want to ensure they have the option to move between sectors and into new employment opportunities within industry.

This means a review of the primacy now given to the statutory placement and finding more ways of involving service users and carers as integral partners in learning. Many voluntary and independent sector organisations are small, unlike statutory authories. This influences the nature of the organisation and the task. Hence in a single day the owner of a small private home, for example, may be involved in such diverse tasks as clearing drains, undertaking staff development of part time workers, providing intimate care for very frail and vulnerable people. This variety is similar in small voluntary agencies.

Increasing specialisation

The generic base of social work is also under challenge. The independent and voluntary sectors have always had a high degree of specialism, but since the implementation of the National Health Service and Community Care and Children Acts there is evidence of increasing specialisation in the statutory sector. Most departments are now divided into children and families and adult care, often with sub-divisions within the latter. Generic training may have been appropriate when there were large social services departments providing services; with the fragmentation of service delivery this is no longer appropriate.

Generic skills remain a foundation for social work, but the way they are used and the additional knowledge required is profoundly influenced by the context of social work practice. The outcome of the Review of the Diploma in Social Work has provided these opportunities. This trend within social work is reinforced by the Scottish/National Vocational Qualification system of qualification, which takes as its focus the specific skills required to undertake a particular job.

One of the challenges to social work education is to ensure that, with this approach to learning which focuses on demonstrating 'on the job skills', the intellectual and research base of social work and social care remains intact. We also have to have new ways of maintaining standards across this fragmented scene and this is the reason why the Implementation Group on the General Social Services Council is recommending the establishment of a Council which will set standards of practice and conduct for practitioners in social work and social care, and hold a register.

Participation and empowerment

The emphasis on participation and empowerment gives priority to different skills. These include information giving, facilitating people's own efforts to describe what their needs are and what they will do to get these met, networking, the capacity to work with innovation and change as an integral part of the job, inventiveness and the ability to focus not solely on the individual but on the wider social network, by promoting and maintaining local groups and support systems.

The emphasis on empowerment is also likely to increase the importance of understanding how adults, including students themselves, learn. Empowerment includes working with people to identify options and corresponding blocks. Essentially this is about learning to cope with new challenges and pressures – learning to go on learning. If there is to be a role for social work in promoting social inclusiveness, the skills required will involve those traditionally associated with community development.

The emphasis on work-based learning as a means of establishing competence

A multiplicity of channels for learning – open/distance, modular, work-based, accreditation of prior learning, staff development – means that the role of the college must also adapt to take these into account. The partnerships already established through the Diploma are an important means by which the role of the academic can be retained within this new framework, where competence to practice is likely to be determined in the workplace.

The task for social services departments is how to manage fragmentation of service providers; for colleges it will be building up working partnerships within this pattern of increasingly diverse employment bases and training needs of social workers

Raising the status of practice

Over the past few years there has been major emphasis in social services departments on getting systems and procedures in place, on taking on new responsibilities for budgeting and for becoming enabling authorities. In the meantime progress on developing practice in order to meet the new social policy requirements has lagged behind in some parts of social services departments, while parts of the voluntary and independent sectors and service user and carer organisations have moved ahead quickly. This is a result of much more than lack of time for experienced staff to be practice teachers, important though this is for the future of social work and social care.

Research carried out by the National Institute for Social Work (Newburn, 1993) and through the Joseph Rowntree Foundation (Marsh and Fisher, 1992) shows that our organisations are not good at learning from what is happening at the front line as a means of developing policy and practice. Supervision is often focused on accountability to the exclusion of learning from and developing practice. The emphasis on individual competence will be to no avail if newly qualified and experienced workers do not also have a 'competent workplace' (Evans and Pottage, 1994) which will both support their competence and learn from the information about front line experience that these staff can contribute to the work of the agency.

Meeting the challenge: Social work education and user involvement

PETER BERESFORD

All change for social work

Social work faces massive change on all sides. This has profound implications for social work education and educators. They are faced with enormous demands, if they are to meet the challenge of the community care revolution. There is a strong temptation to duck the issue and retreat, either to the past or to condemnation of the present. Neither of these courses will help service users or practitioners deal with the demands they now face. Instead social work educators must confront the new times in which they are working. A first step in doing this is to take stock of some of the changes which currently impact upon them.

These are times of fundamental change in social welfare generally, as well as in social work specifically. This is embodied in major shifts in welfare structures, objectives, financing and ideology. It has been reflected in a change of emphasis from public to private; from securing people's rights to emphasising their responsibilities. The pressure for change in welfare cuts across traditional political divisions. Welfare is up for review. The Labour Party's commission on social justice agreed with government that the welfare state must change. Their recipes for the future may be different, but both parties question old, taken-for-granted ideas of universalist services and free services at the point of use. There is now little firm ground or concensus in welfare thinking.

Social work's place within welfare is also changing. It is coming to be more residual, more restricted and, some commentators argue, more regulatory rather than supportive in purpose, with closer control from the centre and fewer resources available at local level.

Social work is itself undergoing considerable change. The National Health Service and Community Care Act and the Children Act altered the legal framework within which social work operates. Service users now have more clearly established rights, as well as responsibilities, some sustained by the force of law. The position, demands and expectations of service users are changing. Service users now formally have a higher profile and more central role in social services policy and practice.

At the same time, organisations and groups of disabled people, psychiatric system survivors, people with learning difficulties, older people, people living with HIV and young people in care, have grown in strength and numbers. Social care service user movements have emerged, mobilised, developed ideas and demands and mounted increasingly effective campaigns to secure their rights and needs.

Since the expansionist days of the 1970s, social work has faced a political climate which its proponents experience at best as neutral, at worst as unsympathetic. All the signs are that in the 1990s this climate has become increasingly hostile. Social work's anti-oppressive and pro-equality value base has not fitted well with the shift to the right in British politics and public life. The on-going catalogue of public inquiries, tragedies and cases of abuse also continues to undermine public confidence in a profession which has never benefited from the deference attached to other more traditional, male dominated professions.

The constraints operating on social work's own institutions

At the same time, social work's own organisations and institutions have come under increasing financial and ideological pressure and constraints. The Central Council for Education and Training in Social Work has been attacked for its commitment to anti-oppressive practice, and its management profile reviewed in the light of government priorities. The British Association of Social Work continues to be characterised by a small and ageing membership and a weak public profile.

Despite a long record of expertise in social work and social services and current record of positive partnerships with service users and their organisations, the National Institute for Social Work must increasingly rely on competing for contracts with the growing number of private consultancies. The Race Equality Unit, despite its major role and contribution, faces the same problems of inadequate and uncertain funding which restrict the activities of Black and minority ethnic organisations more generally.

Renewed calls for a general social work council have attracted little public interest or support, or met a less than enthusiastic response from government and raised the question of whether its primary purpose is with safegarding the rights and needs of professionals or of service users. In this downbeat context, the demise of social work's own weekly journal *Social Work Today* in the early 1990s comes to have a more symbolic significance.

There have always been gaps and differences between the skills formally taught for social practice and the skills actually used and needed. Both have now changed. Both now demand new skills, knowledge, understanding, philosophies and values. At the same time, there are strong fears among some social work commentators that there has been a move to a more technicist approach to practice which denies its essentially political and reforming nature (Jones, 1994/5).

It is not even clear, as we write, what if any future social work has, or whether it even has a continuing clear identity of its own. Significantly the Griffiths Report made no mention of social work. Workers from other backgrounds and professions, such as therapists, nurses and care workers, are now seen as equally suitable candidates to take on the new care management tasks and responsibilities currently required of social workers. Meanwhile many of the tasks traditionally associated with social work, such as developing relationships with service users, counselling and advocacy – even if they were not always the reality of day to day practice in statutory services – have been whittled away to occupy even less place on agencies' and government agendas for practice.

The role of training and education in response to change

So social work is operating at a time of constant and enormous change. Some of these changes may be positive, but many are experienced as negative. This is a time of enormous uncertainty and instability in human services, when there is a strong sense on both sides of the welfare counter that public policy and provision has been destabilised.

But it is also important to avoid nostalgia and to be wary of any tendency to hark back to 'better times'. Social work's resources, tasks and agenda may have seemed clearer and more secure to educators and practitioners in other times. But writing as a social work educator *and* service user, I feel obliged to offer a reminder that for service users there was no golden age of social work.

Social work education and training clearly have a pivotal part to play in dealing with the changes which are now affecting social work. They must play this part at a time when they have themselves also been subject to radical change in both philosophy and operation. Perhaps the sharpest expression of the role education and training have to play here is in negotiating the disabling tension which exists between the two government principles officially and rhetorically driving policy and practice. These are the principles of:

• value for money

• consumer choice and involvement.

The government has consistently expressed its commitment to both. If the Audit Commission was established as the guardian of the first, legal requirements for consultation, redress and a greater role for non-statutory provision have been offered as the guarantee of the second. But there are two problems here. First the official assumption seems to have been that here were two horses pulling in the same direction. But these two principles are as likely to be in conflict as complementary. Money and need have rarely been comfortable harnessed together. Then there is the issue of getting the balance right. John Bowis, as minister with responsibility for community care, has himself acknowledged this issue: "Community care is sometimes more geared to resources than needs. It has to be both, doesn't it?" (Bowis, 1994).

Local authority social services departments have repeatedly reported inadequate levels of funding since the implementation of the community care reforms. Service users and carers report the same problem (Beresford, 1995). If value for money becomes code for tight budgetary constraints, then conflict between it and consumer choice is likely to mean budget-driven policy and practice over-riding the aspiration for user-led services.

The crucial role that education and training has to play is to equip and empower workers and students to act effectively with and for service users and carers in such a scenario. If practitioners are going to be able to cope effectively with the pressures and restraints operating on them, and work appropriately to meet the rights and needs of service users, they will need to be equipped with appropriate knowledge, skills and understanding. Otherwise they are likely to be immobilised, incapacitated and disempowered.

There has been growing discussion of the need for community care practitioners themselves to be empowered, if they are to support the empowerment of service users (Stevenson and Parsloe, 1993). Training is vital in this. Clearly it is not an alternative to ensuring adequate resourcing and priority for community care policy and provision. But until these are guaranteed, practitioners will find themselves trying to mediate the effects of inadequate policy and provision, to do the best for service users and carers. This is a difficult task, which may sometimes feel impossible. Training which helps practitioners and managers recognise and negotiate the conflicts between resource limits and meeting people's needs is crucial here.

The obstacles facing social work education

Responding to this challenge is clearly no small order for social work education and training. It is also a task which it may not be strongly placed to deal with. There are a number of reasons for this. Staff in academic institutions are an ageing population. All the indications are that few have first hand experience of practice under the new arrangements for community care. Some teaching institutions have sought to address this by developing part-time and joint appointments and short-term secondments, which enable staff to maintain an invaluable two-way traffic between their practice and teaching.

But social work has generally failed to develop organisational and career structures which make it possible for workers to maintain practice and promotion when moving into management, education and training. College courses mostly rely on 'guest speakers' and placements to provide such input, but this also often serves to emphasise and reinforce the gaps and inconsistencies between schools and agencies. Accelerating rates of change in modern social services mean that many teachers are having to rely on a stock of direct experience which may have limited relevance to current demands and conditions. This is particularly true for the professors and other senior staff who set both departmental and educational agendas.

There is also other growing pressure away from an emphasis on practice and work with students. The university expansion programme and the ending of polytechnic and higher education institution status has put an increasing pressure on social work departments and individual members of staff to publish and undertake research. While this may be valuable, without additional resources it is difficult to see how they can maintain their commitment to practice and student learning.

Social work educators are further disadvantaged by their location in an educational system which isn't geared to and doesn't always recognise the particular need for resources and higher staff ratios which social work requires. It is also a system which itself faces growing problems of inadequate and insecure funding and a pressing need to generate income. As a result, social work educators are looking to offer more post-qualification and academic courses, which may meet their financial needs but leave the basic training issues posed by broader social work change unresolved. The long term future of social work education is becoming increasingly unclear and uncertain.

User involvement: finding a way forward

The scale of change and uncertainty facing social work trainers and educators, and the obstacles in their way in trying to deal with it, may leave them feeling battered, confused and unclear about how they are to negotiate their way through the community care revolution. I want to argue here that *user involvement* – a key concept and development which has been given force by the community care reforms – can offer them a way forward.

The community care reforms were underpinned by a variety of different, often competing aspirations and ideological commitments. We have seen the government's emphasis on two principles, consumer choice and involvement and value for money, which have often seemed contradictory in theory and antithetical in practice.

The *creative* impetus of the reforms has come from the idea of user involvement. It has caught the imagination of service users, carers, practitioners and educators alike. It provides the philosophical and practical basis for qualitatively different policy and provision. On the ground, it has been the driving force for the many positive developments and initiatives which have followed in the wake of the National Health Service and Community Care Act. Whereas government emphasis on value for money and cost-effectiveness has generally been experienced by service users and practitioners as a check on innovation and change, user involvement has emerged as a rallying cry for them.

User involvement underlies every aspect of both organisational reform and service process and provision heralded by the reforms. There is agreement about the importance of involvement irrespective of political position and across both sides of the community care counter. The government's market-led model of community care rhetorically prioritises and legitimates the public consumer and end-user, for all its ambiguity. The disabled people's and social care service users' movements demand people's involvement in all aspects of defining and meeting their wants and needs and provide it with a real force for change.

While it would be naive to suggest that there is any agreed definition of user involvement and that everyone uses the term in the same way, it has generally been a force for positive change. User involvement represents both the means and ends for the needs-led services to which the government has committed itself and which service users are demanding with more and more authority.

A user-led model of social work

The idea of user involvement helps us to make the move to a different model of social work and social work practice. This draws us on to some of the themes which Daphne Statham raises elsewhere in this book. User involvement predicates a model of social work which has both coherence and authority. It is a model which is associated with two key themes. These themes are first, *social inclusion* and second, *autonomy and interdependence*. As Bill Jordan argued twenty years ago, social work has tended to be typified by the making of separate inferior provision for disadvantaged, disempowered groups, creating and reinforcing their isolation and dependence (Jordan, 1975). If anything, this is a tendency which the political right's residual approach to welfare and social work is likely to reinforce rather than reduce, with its emphasis on 'targeting' and minimal state intervention. The model for practice, including social work practice, which emerges from disabled people's and service users' critiques and which user involvement helps to make possible, is one which takes as its objectives people's social inclusion and the enabling of autonomy and independent living through the provision of adequate and appropriate support.

We can now begin to see how user involvement becomes central to social work education and training. It is central to the government's community care reforms. It is both an implicit and explicit demand of the disabled people's and social care service users' movements. It is a principle and goal of a model of social work practice which is consistent with both of these.

User involvement and social work education

This discussion is crucially about the part that social work education and training have to play in negotiating the community care revolution. If they are to play their part in this by equipping practitioners with the skills for user involvement and extending user involvement in social work practice, policy and provision, they must first address user involvement themselves. This needs to be done in three key areas of social work education and training. These are:

- the provision of teaching, training and education
- the process of education and training
- the subject matter of education and training.

Detailed guidance on all of these is available from CCETSW's national consultation on user involvement in social work education (Beresford, 1994).

1. User involvement in the provision of education and training

There is increasing recognition of the importance of user involvement in the provision of social work education and training. It is now happening more often in training and educational establishments. There is now increasing use of service user trainers on courses. But this involvement is often ad hoc, patchy and badly done. A number of personal and institutional obstacles stand in its way, notably the imbalance of power between educators and service users and the lack of a strong tradition of involvement in social work education.

The CCETSW consultation highlighted the need for a range of supports for user involvement to flourish in the provision of training. Both educators and service users need such support. The support which educators needs includes:

- knowing how best to work with and support the involvement of service users
- ways of addressing traditions of under-valuing and discriminating against service users
- building links with service users and their organisations to foster networks and networking with them
- ways of learning about and understanding the histories, aims and philosophies of service users' organisations and movements.

Support for service users is also needed in a number of areas. These include support to take part. This entails:

- information provided in accessible and appropriate formats
- costs for personal assistance, facilitators, supporters and transport provided without question
- equal pay and conditions.

Service users sum up such support as reflecting a valuing of them, their contribution and their expertise. They also seek support in terms of training. This includes:

- opportunities to be effective trainers and educators on the basis that everyone needs such training, including service user trainers
- anti-discrimination training
- the development of training courses and qualifications for service user trainers.

Service users and their organisations have already done much work to develop such 'training for trainers', and produced their own training materials, with the accent on service users training service users. But clearly there is also a role here for academic and educational organisations supporting and certificating this work.

Service users also need support to develop their own independent organisations and groups. While the number of such groups has grown rapidly in recent years, there are still some areas without user-led organisations, or without organisations of particular groups of service users, and such organisations face persistent problems of inadequate and insecure funding. At the same time, they have played a crucial role in the development of user involvement in training. This extends to providing:

• a key source of service user trainers

• a basis for representation, through their democratic structures.

Support for disabled people's and service users' organisations in social work education and training should be seen as part of a broader strategy of supporting and encouraging such organisations.

Support is also needed to involve Black and minority ethnic group service users trainers. This includes support for:

• Black and minority ethnic group service user trainers and their organisations to gain skills and get involved

• disabled people's and service users' organisations to reach out more effectively to include Black and minority ethnic service users and user trainers.

2. User involvement in the process of social work education and training

The CCETSW consultation with service users highlighted their desire to by *fully* and *systematically* involved in the process of social work training. Service users are used to being consulted after key decisions have been made and being expected to slot into pre-existing arrangements. This is generally experienced as inadequate and unacceptable. Service users are increasingly reluctant just to be tagged on to existing training, asked to offer isolated sessions, to provide 'user input' and to be one-off guest speakers. Instead they want a real say in training. They also make clear that user involvement isn't only needed in the classroom or educational institution, but must also extend to placements and practice learning. Service users and their organisations want to be involved at a variety of levels. They want to be involved in:

- and informed about the planning of specific courses to which they are invited to contribute
- planning the curriculum and curriculum development
- planning methods of study
- course and student assessment and standard setting
- the education departments and agencies.

As the service users CCETSW consulted said, for this to happen requires the development of forums for discussion and decision-making which are sensitive to and supportive of the involvement of service users. Service users are calling for a new kind of partnership in social work education and the recognition of another partner in the process of education and training. This is beginning to happen. There are individual instances of such progressive collaborative developments which prove they are feasible and effective. Service users' organisations are beginning to provide placements, supervise students and become members of Diploma in Social Work partnerships. But such initiatives are still few and far between. Coherent policy for user involvement in the process of training and education is still largely a goal for the future.

3. User involvement as a subject of study

In addition to ensuring user involvement in the provision and process of training, it should be fully covered as a subject of training. As well as being addressed specifically in training, it should also be one of the themes running through it. To cover user involvement fully will require exploring both what user involvement means and how to support and encourage it in practice. Service user trainers are likely to have an important part to play here in developing this major theme and area of study in social work training.

The CCETSW consultation on service user involvement in social work education highlighted three particular areas to be included in developing learning on user involvement. These were:

- to take full account of the growing body of material produced by disabled people and service users themselves in the curriculum and giving equal weight to it in reading and resource lists

- to include ideas and theories developed by disabled people and service users, for example the social model of disability; ideas of independent living and mental distress; and taking full account of service users' perspectives in theory building

- to take proper account of the new emancipatory and participatory research approaches developed by disabled people and service users in research training: there is a growing emphasis on research in social work education, both for educators and students, and these new methodologies emphasise a changed, more equal social relation in research production which has particular relevance for social work research.

Broader issues of user involvement

User involvement raises broader issues of equal opportunities and discrimination and also needs to be related to them. It should not be treated in isolation as an academic exercise, but constantly be related to and monitored against anti-discrimination and equal opportunities policies. Integrating user involvement in this way will take many expressions. These include:

- developing equal access to social work education and training for people who are disabled and service users

- developing equal access and ensuring equal opportunities for disabled people and service users to be social work educators

- highlighting the importance of user involvement where social work practice is concerned with restrictions on people's rights, to ensure that these rights are fully safeguarded

- recognising and encouraging the overlaps that exist between educators and service users: educators and students should be encouraged to explore the overlapping oppressions they share with service users on grounds of age, race, gender, disability, class and sexual identity and to question any ideas of a hierarchy of oppression.

A strategy for change

In this discussion, I have argued that the idea and practice of user involvement offers educators a way of meeting the challenge of the community care revolution. As we have seen, there is support for the idea from both government and service user movements. There is now considerable experience and expertise, particularly among the disabled people's and social care service users' movements, about how to do it. But if it is to be developed coherently and effectively in social work education and training there need to be strategies and policies for its implementation. Otherwise we will continue to see it develop in a patchy and uneven way. Such a strategy needs to develop at all levels, with individual teachers and departments, at local, regional and national levels. Service users need to be fully involved in the development of such a strategy. It means the opening up of discussions between service users' organisations and educators.

As we have seen, the community care revolution has made new demands on practice and called for new practice skills. Two recent initiatives have taken the discussion even further by involving service users and carers themselves in identifying the skills and standards which are needed for community care practice (Beresford and Trevillion, 1995; Harding and Beresford, 1995). This is what user-led and needs-led policy and provision is ultimately about. Social work training and education have a unique opportunity to be in the vanguard of this development. It offers both them and service users the real prospect of a positive future.

Advocacy and equity

KATH GILLESPIE SELLS

Equity

The delivery of social care raises two fundamental issues: who receives services and how appropriate they are. The fact that services have traditionally been and are still largely resource-led rather than needs-led makes issues of fairness and how the cake is cut particularly important.

With the steady growth of the disabled people's movement and the seeking of users' views, there has been a move towards user involvement at many stages of the process from the planning to delivery of services. The introduction of new legislation and the reorganisation of social services departments has brought opportunities as well as challenges. Care management could be considered a way of controlling budget-led services and creatively providing services that service users want and need. However, there appears to be much frantic and unproductive activity which is largely reactive rather than proactive.

Discussion about terminology and the training needs of care managers, along with the requirements to manage budgets and work with other agencies, seems to dominate debate about these changes, with the quality and relevance of services rarely making the agenda.

Organisations have responded variously to the need to involve service users. Some have taken this opportunity to include users' views seriously and provide services which are user-influenced if not user-led. Others listen to service users and decide to include what is convenient or easily incorporated into existing plans. Equity can only be achieved through meaningful, systematic consultation and a willingness to change practice in the light of users' views. However, before this stage is reached, there has to be a recognition of the power imbalance between service users and service providers. Social services staff express their feelings of demoralisation and powerlessness in the face of major change after major change. However, social workers do have power, and however enlightened or dedicated to change for the better they are all-powerful to service users, who must depend on service provision for their very survival.

However, power need not necessarily be corrupting or damaging. Users of services need powerful allies to ensure positive, productive change takes place. The very existence of power need not mean that the 'haves' retain power and the 'have nots' remain powerless. Real equality is about power sharing. It is about professionals recognising that they have much to gain from empowering service users to express their real feelings about current provision and to make suggestions for improvement. Professionals have sometimes seen acknowledging that services users are experts in their own right as an inevitably de-skilling process, rather than recognising that there are many new skills to be learned and existing skills to be updated and improved in the ever-changing field of social care.

Just as social workers have demonstrated a reluctance to move toward real user involvement and the desired goal of user-led services, likewise social work educators often feel threatened at the suggestion of service user trainers' involvement in curriculum design and delivery. Many obstacles are presented to avoid user trainers, for example who is a representative user and how do you work in partnership with user trainers? Even payment of user trainers has been presented as a problem to be resolved before involving the real experts in the education process of tomorrow's social workers.

Other concerns of education include the lack of uniformity of approach in curriculum development, limited networking between education establishments, resources developed in isolation and the common problem of a lack of user groups from which to find user trainers. However legitimate these problems, in many establishments they are used as obstacles to real change and as a validation of existing conservative practices. Other educational establishments are more honest and state that there really is no room in an already full curriculum for equality issues, believing that the delivery of social care by sensitive individuals will result in sensitivity and equality.

Achieving equity and equality in social care services demands effective user involvement. It means challenging discrimination on grounds of age, race, disability, gender and sexuality. If equality is not considered of major importance in social work education, reasons will always be seen why educators should not start the process. Equality is not a luxury topic to be left off the agenda at will. Discrimination exists; few would dispute this, or that education has an important role in challenging discrimination. Yet equality training is still often viewed as an optional extra, a luxury when the basics have been covered. Until equality is integrated throughout the curriculum, educators will compound discrimination by sending social work students into situations where they lack awareness and are ill-prepared to challenge oppressive practices.

Not knowing where to start or not having all the answers to complex questions is no reason to put aside equality issues in the curriculum. Trained user trainers and consultants can legitimately represent users' views. It is time to take up the challenge of change and work with user trainers to provide social care students with a curriculum that prepares then for the real world and puts them directly in touch with service users who are empowered and opinionated. This in itself can be very challenging to the traditional client/professional relationship.

Advocacy

There is still a great deal of confusion around the issue of advocacy. If we acknowledge the existence of racism and disablism in this society, those acting as advocates on behalf of Black and disabled people have a particularly challenging task in ensuring that discrimination does not result in inadequate or inappropriate service provision. Add to this already charged and complex issue of discrimination the fact that some service users belong to more than one oppressed minority, and ensuring equality in the advocacy process becomes a harder task and greater achievement. A Black person provided with a service that is culturally sensitive will still be oppressed if they have to hide their sexuality because the service provider is homophobic. Stereotypes and assumptions inform many decisions taken on behalf of service users. If we have equality policies and anti-discriminatory practices in place, designed to meet the needs of all clients, incidents of disadvantage and discrimination will be reduced.

Whether social workers are best placed to be care managers and whether social workers can be service users' advocates as well as care managers are issues of continuing concern. Community care legislation has placed social workers in the market place with the unfamiliar roles of purchasers and providers of care. There is also a requirement to work with and alongside other professionals in the health, independent and voluntary sectors, to obtain the best possible package of care for service users. However, social workers are also the gatekeepers to such services and ultimately decide who receives services and who does not. This may also be influenced by managers or personal career opportunities.

This role conflict is one of the most worrying aspects of care management confronting service users and their organisations. There is no legislation to protect disabled people from the worst effects of discrimination, and it would appear that even though there is a duty upon local authorities to assess need, there is no legislation to enforce the provision of services to meet that need. This is just one among many examples of the exercise of power by social workers that could result in inequality and discrimination.

Use instead of an independent advocate would ensure the service user receives the best possible package of services appropriate to their need. There is no division of loyalty between employer and service user. The independent advocate does not have to consider others who may also need services. Service users are often told that if they receive more personal assistance, then other service users will receive less. Placing the responsibility and ultimate decision with the service user in this way is not the kind of 'involvement' services users need or want.

Educators who are concerned about retaining core values in social work and who want to include issues of equality and advocacy in the curriculum, but are concerned about preparing social workers for work in the real world, should recognise that these are one and the same issue. The real test of an understanding of equity, fairness and advocacy is in their interpretation when dealing with service users. The challenge to social workers and social work educators is to be prepared to adapt to changing times, to be sensitive to changing social need and adjust their practice to meet it. Care management and advocacy are just such challenges, and social work educators need to recognise that there is already the expertise to meet this challenge. They need look no further than service users and their organisations, who are involved on a daily basis with issues of equity and advocacy. Many service users are advocates for other service users both formally and informally. An expertise has been developed.

Perhaps the greatest challenge is one of attitude: can social work educators recognise that there is no room for the paternalism of the past, that out of necessity disabled people and their organisations have developed a body of knowledge that could benefit the social work profession? Can social work educators lay aside notions of professionalism and fears of power-sharing and deskilling and grapple with the nettle of face to face dialogue with users of services?

Conclusion

Unless equality is a central concern to all social work practitioners and educators alike, on what basis will social work staff confronted with limited resources allocate resources? Will this be based on age, race, gender or other discrimination? How do educators prepare trainees for such dilemmas?

Disabled people and their organisations insist on involvement in the planning and delivery of services. What happens if staff consult and do not like what they are told? Who is going to challenge their employer because their clients are going without essential assistance because they cannot afford to pay? What do social workers do with the challenge that disabled people's very existence keeps non-disabled people in work? How will educators keep tomorrow's social workers from breaking down? In such a changing and often hostile environment, how do we ensure social workers don't become so demoralised that they are no longer the powerful allies we need?

In seeking answers to these complex questions we often only reveal more. However, part answers and solutions are being found all the time by service users, often out of desperate and immediate need. By involving them more fully as user trainers and consultants, social work educators will find ways of addressing issues of advocacy and equity and challenging discrimination.

Empowerment and user involvement

JAN WALLCRAFT

Re-examining the role of social work within community care, and the kind of training and education social workers should be receiving to prepare them for that role, is a valuable opportunity to look at the poor image social workers have had among the recipients of their services.

Poor and working class people of all races have tended to be deeply suspicious of social workers, and to regard them as a kind of moral police, agents of the state, and as middle-class professionals, out of touch with their everyday realities. As a recipient of services, both as a former mental patient and as a parent with a school phobic child, I have personally experienced social work intervention that has been helpful and, sometimes from the same people, frustatingly inappropriate and insensitive.

The only way for social work practice to begin to reflect truly the interests of its recipients is to involve them and their organisations in the training and education of social workers. If this does not happen, social work in community care will simply repeat the mistakes of the past or fall into new errors. Defending and professionalising social work should not be at the expense of the recipients. Good social work practice must mean providing a service that users want. The only way to ensure this is to ask them and involve them fully.

Social workers' roles have gradually changed since the foundation of the welfare state. Social workers have always been subject to criticism from all sides. They have been expected to take on and solve the social problems of industrial society and then post-industrial society. It is their job to soften the impact of massive social changes, to make up for society's shortcomings and injustices, root out and prevent abuse and violence. Of course they cannot help but fail often at this task, and thus become a convenient object of blame from the media, public and politicians. It is an almost impossible job.

As government welfare policies change, so the roles of social workers have to change, and social workers and their organisations must adapt and try to protect their position and their jobs. Any group of workers does the same. However as with many other groups of workers, in protecting their position social workers have rarely thought to make alliances with the less powerful and lower paid care workers. They have signally failed to build alliances with the users of their services. Instead they have responded by distancing themselves, transforming social work into a profession and building a mystique about social work skills.

Now that we are departing from the old ways of providing social care directly by municipal workers, care work is being passed back to the community itself or to the independent or voluntary sectors. The position of social workers is changing, and by professionalising they have been able to corner some benefits from the changes. Social workers have stood for a social model of care and have vied for power with medical professionals. To some extent, in the era of community care they have succeeded in raising their status, particularly in mental health services, as Approved Social Workers. The social model of care has gained at the expense of medical care in large institutions. But at the same time the role of social workers has begun to change from care providers to care managers, assessors of needs which will be met by others, often in more lowly and insecure jobs. Social workers have advanced themselves in relation to those providing direct caring, such as home care workers.

However those of us on the receiving end of services have always been the last to be asked what kind of services we want. Though we have watched horrified as government has taken apart the welfare state, we are beginning to see that the Thatcher legacy has its beneficial side. Along with the dumping of the aim to provide services 'from the cradle to the grave', we are seeing the gradual, or at least the potential demise of paternalistic assumptions about what people need or ought to need. New debates have opened up about consultation, consumerism, choice, user involvement, participation, needs-led services.

Though much of this may be only rhetoric, there have been real opportunities for empowerment to happen, for users to begin to act as advocates, development workers, trainers, public speakers, researchers, and even service providers. We are sitting on committees at local, regional and national levels, putting forward our views, not only on the type of service we want, but the style in which we want to see those services delivered. The key word is empowerment. We no longer want services which expect us to be passive, dependent, grateful, quiet and well-behaved. We want services which enable us to be who we are, and to live the best lives we can. We want rights, not patronage.

Social workers and social work educators will miss this development at their peril. Service users have not on the whole experienced their relationships with social workers as empowering. We have tended to view social workers as controlling, pathologising, victim-blaming, out of touch with our lives. In the book of the MIND People First survey *Experiencing Psychiatry* (Rogers, Pilgrim and Lacey, 1993) social workers were rated by patients as second to psychiatrists as the group who were regarded as least helpful by psychiatric in-patients.

The professionalisation of social work may have raised the status, improved qualifications and ethical standards of work, but if users are not involved, social work practice will continue to be alienating, disempowering, insensitive and paternalistic to its recipients, and ultimately will not be successful in helping communities to manage the new burdens of coping and caring with less residential provision , and reduced housing benefits. The best way to counter this is for service users to be involved in planning the training, delivering it and helping to asess social work trainees.

Social workers and their organisations must become the allies of service users and user groups. It is time for them to listen and learn, to demystify their practice, to become more sensitive to issues of race, gender and social class, to find empowering ways to work; to own up to their own personal and work role limitations; to value their own personal experience of feeling disempowered, as children and as users of services, as a source of identification with users – instead of valuing text book learning and paper qualifications.

Social workers should not try to imitate psychoanalytic psychotherapists, but should learn instead to value the more humane and down-to-earth skills of counselling, emotional support, non-judgmental listening, information giving, facilitating, networking and advocacy, which are what service users want.

Groups who are the most socially disadvantaged, such as old people, mental patients, people with long term needs for support, tend to lose out also in getting the social work help they want. Racist assumptions are often made by social services about Black families' abilities to care for their children, or about Asian families' lack of need for services. Although there has been more emphasis on equal opportunities in social work education of late, it will only be when all these groups are properly and directly represented in training and education programmes for social workers that these prejudices will be fully eradicated.

With the challenging of welfarism, we are learning to help ourselves and speak for ourselves, and despite all the problems of inadequate and inappropriate services, there are advantages and opportunities. If we can prevent the community care revolution from being a desperate scramble for diminishing resources and transform it into an exercise in rebuilding our communities and support networks, we may yet have cause for celebration. Social workers can join that work or continue to distance themselves behind boundaries of professionalism and engage in power struggles with other professional groups. Social work educators have a vital role in offering new generations of social workers an opportunity to confront reality. It is no use for social workers to continue pretending to be able to do the impossible, to provide houses, jobs and benefits that don't exist. It is time for them to cease hiding their inability to solve people's practical or emotional problems behind empty therapeutic jargon, and become genuine allies of the people in their communities.

The importance of including mental health system survivors in Approved Social Work training

MIRIAM HASTINGS

In December 1992 I was approached by National MIND to research and write a resource pack for mental health system survivors taking part in Approved Social Work training. This pack was originally commisioned by the Central Council for Education and Training in Social Work, recognising how important it is for mental health service users to contribute to Approved Social Work training programmes. The purpose of the pack was to give advice, ideas, and information on every aspect of Approved Social Work training for the use of service users/survivors planning to take part in such training.

I worked on the pack with a co-worker, David Crepaz-Keay, then Chair of Survivors Speak Out. While doing the research, we interviewed interested people from a wide range of backgrounds, including service users, user trainers, Approved Social Workers and Approved Social Work trainees (including some who had been trained by survivors and some who hadn't) and Approved Social Work training co-ordinators. We interviewed women and men from a variety of cultural backgrounds, living in both rural and metropolitan areas.

We wanted to address issues around equality that are often overlooked or ignored in mental health services, from the perspective that Approved Social Work training courses must acknowledge and, in turn, address issues of race, culture, gender, sexuality, disability and other areas of social oppression that are rife in the mental health system, and our main findings do indeed emphasise the need for user trainers to be directly involved in training Approved Social Workers.

Equality issues

It is all too easy for someone to be labelled as mentally ill because their behaviour or their appearance doesn't conform to the expectations of mental health professionals. Service users who have suffered from this kind of discrimination are in the best position to enable Approved Social Work trainees to question their own stereotyped and prejudiced assumptions and expectations.

The definition of mental health and mentally healthy behaviour is set up and maintained by a predominantly white, male, middle class, heterosexist, eurocentric psychiatric profession which reflects the dominant values of society. What is considered mentally healthy and acceptable or understandable behaviour in men is not viewed as such in women. Equally, it is impossible to make an accurate diagnosis across cultural barriers. White mental health professionals often interpret differences in lifestyle and culture as symptoms of mental illness. A white eurocentric psychiatrist will be ignorant of ways of behaviour or self-expression that are common and even expected in African-Caribbean or Asian cultures. Moreover, a cultural heritage of oppression determines a view of such people as different, abnormal, inadequate and inferior by those with power and authority over them.

Here it is vitally important that Approved Social Workers are made aware of gender and racial and cultural stereotyping, both in society and within the mental health system, since Approved Social Workers need to combat the effects of stereotyping and discrimination in every area of their work. User trainers from marginalised and oppressed cultural backgrounds and experiences are able to convey and communicate this need more effectively and with more insight than any theoretical teaching can do.

Approved Social Workers need to be taught to look at people in their wider social context, not as psychiatric 'cases', and to be sensitive always to the possibility that the person has been labelled as 'mentally ill' because of other people's prejudice and ignorance. It is equally important that Approved Social Workers realise how crucial it is that they should always be aware of any possible prejudice in themselves that will affect their ability to assess fairly a person's mental state and real needs, and that they should always be honest and thorough in scrutinising their own responses and attitudes to any individual referred to them for assessment, in order to avoid any unconscious discrimination against the person.

This applies to discrimination caused by ignorance as well as that stemming from hostile prejudice. Approved Social Workers need to be taught to recognise their own ignorance of other groups in society, and to understand the importance of both acknowledging that ignorance and attempting to overcome it. The best way to overcome ignorance and to combat prejudice is to learn from the individual concerned. When assessing a person for possible admission to hospital, the Approved Social Worker must find out that person's own view of what is happening to them and why it is happening. They should listen to the person with attention and respect, and if the person needs an interpreter or a signer, ensure that one is found who can really advocate for them (not a relative or neighbour!). Where any cultural or gender differences exist, or other differences in experience that are unfamiliar to the Approved Social Worker, they should always find out from the individual concerned how they see their experience and what it feels like.

Approved Social Workers are far more likely to carry out good practice such as this if they have been trained about these issues by the people most concerned and who have direct experience.

Effects of being sectioned

It is extremely important that Approved Social Work trainees are taught to realise fully the consequences of sectioning an individual, since the effects of being compulsorily admitted to hospital on a section are profound and devastating, in both the short and long term.

The experience of being forced to go into hospital and to receive treatment against their will often makes a person feel they have completely lost their identity – they're no longer the same person, but someone everyone else is seeing as 'mentally ill'. They are suddenly denied all control over what happens to them and put in an extremely powerless, confusing and terrifying position. This has a profoundly damaging long term emotional effect.

Being sectioned immediately affects every aspect of their lives, such as their families, their relationships and their whole place in society. Many people lose their jobs and often their homes through being sectioned, and also their partners and friends. Unfortunately the stigma of being sectioned often affects the attitudes of those closest to the person, as well as the attitudes of employers, work colleagues, landlords and neighbours.

People frequently leave hospital after several months having to face all the social consequences and stigma of having been sectioned, with little or no follow-up support. Many of the people we interviewed had received no practical help in terms of housing, claiming benefits, occupation or employment. Mothers who are sectioned often have their children taken into care, and usually find it agonisingly difficult to get them back and reunite their families. It is important that Approved Social Work trainees are taught to keep closely in touch with someone they have sectioned, giving them support at every stage, including after discharge from hospital. It seems that all too often Approved Social Workers sign section papers – frequently after interviewing someone who is far too drugged to be able to talk to them and so to be accurately assessed – and then are never seen by the sectioned person again.

The effects of being sectioned can be prolonged and very damaging in terms of confidence, social relationships and future job prospects. The individual is usually faced with the choice of either hiding the fact that they have been sectioned from prospective employers, new friends they meet and possible partners, or telling the truth and facing prejudice and probable rejection. And if they don't tell the truth, they have to live with the stress of fearing they will be found out and penalised for their discretion. People who have been sectioned have to live with the stigma for the rest of their lives.

Accepting alternative viewpoints

It is very important that Approved Social Workers realise how much they need to listen to people in distress and crisis – even when the person doesn't appear able to talk rationally or coherently, it is vital that mental health professionals listen to them. Constant communication needs to be maintained, and this can only be done if the Approved Social Worker involved is prepared to spend time listening to the person respectfully, trying to empathise with them and to enter their experience. It is also only possible to communicate with someone who is not drugged-up. Approved Social Workers should adamantly refuse to assess people for sectioning who have been so medicated that they cannot talk. The person's account of what is happening to them should be respected and taken seriously. Then usually the most bizarre behaviour or incoherent statements begin to make some sense and become easier to understand.

It is also important for Approved Social Workers to realise that experiences that aren't recognised as 'normal' by the majority of society, such as hearing voices or seeing visions, aren't necessarily a problem or a sign of disturbance or 'illness'. Many people hear voices without this causing them difficulties or disrupting their lives. The Approved Social Worker should accept the individual's judgement as to whether they find these experiences a problem. If the person is bothered by hearing voices, the Approved Social Worker should spend time talking with them, trying to understand what the voices mean – not immediately assume that the person needs admitting to hospital. Sometimes people can learn a lot about what's really causing their distress from listening to their voices. They should be treated with respect.

This also applies to apparently bizarre behaviour, for example behaviour that might be dismissed as paranoid. If the Approved Social Worker spends time entering into the person's experience and understanding it, they may well find that the person's behaviour makes a lot of sense. So-called 'paranoid' behaviour is often caused by perfectly rational fears. If a person's relatives or partner, for example, are conspiring with mental health profes- sionals to admit the person to hospital against their will, they are inevitably going to make the person feel threatened and perse- cuted – this is hardly a delusion.

Alternatives to sectioning

Under the 1983 Mental Health Act, Approved Social Workers are required to consider alternatives to compulsory admission where possible. This means that Approved Social Workers need to know what community resources are available outside the hospital and to be aware of the importance of making full use of them. Approved Social Workers have a personal responsibility to ensure that an individual is not sectioned unless there really is no alternative.

Users we interviewed felt that Approved Social Workers should take a holistic approach towards a person they are assessing, looking at the person's whole life situation, and that they should work towards making the medical professionals recognise the social problems of the individuals and not just pathologise the individual's distress. It is important that Approved Social Workers listen to the person they are assessing. They should find out from the person what support systems they have, if any, in the community, and what services they think would help them to get through their crisis. Approved Social Workers will be far more likely to adopt good practice if they have been made aware of such issues by user trainers while still training to be Approved Social Workers, or even better, while doing their basic social work training.

Many of the users we spoke to stressed the damage being sectioned does to people, the importance of preventing people reaching such a critical stage that they need hospital admission, and suggested ways that severe mental crisis might be avoided or alleviated. Alternatives to hospital are needed because the hospital system is often very damaging to people, in addition to the social stigma attached to being sectioned. It is extremely important that Approved Social Work trainees recognise that compulsory admissions to hospital happen far too frequently and needlessly, and often lead to the devastation and ruin people's lives.

Language and disempowerment

Specialised jargonistic language has the effect of making people who are unfamiliar with it feel confused, powerless and inferior. Professionals often use jargon, sometimes because they are so accustomed to it that they forget other people aren't, and sometimes deliberately to make themselves feel more secure in their professional role. This kind of language works to disempower people by denying them the information about what is happening to them that they need. When carrying out sectioning procedures, it is particularly important that Approved Social Workers talk in simple, jargon-free language, both to the individual being sectioned and when talking to others in front of that individual.

Once again, training on social work courses carried out by user trainers would help to teach social work trainees the importance of using understandable, accessible, clear and respectful language. While the use of jargon and specialist language is disempowering, it is just as damaging and harmful to deny people access to the means of communication that they need to express themselves. A person with a hearing impairment, for example, who has difficulty communicating verbally should always be provided with someone who can use sign language and can act as their advocate. Equally, where English isn't a person's first language a sympathetic interpreter should always be present. Even if the individual usually speaks very good English, it must be remembered that it will be much harder for them to communicate in a foreign language when they are distressed; and if someone is in danger of being sectioned, it is vitally important that they aren't put under greater strain and more disadvantages.

Approved Social Work trainees need to be made aware of the importance of always treating people with honesty, openness, and respect, and need to be trained in giving people all the information available, in language that can be easily understood, as well as ensuring that the information is entirely correct and accurate.

If Approved Social Work trainees are trained by user trainers who have experienced compulsory admissions on section, they will learn that people in crisis are ordinary people, the same as themselves, and as a result treat people when they are going through crisis with more respect and sensitivity.

Quasi-markets in welfare*

JULIAN LE GRAND

Introduction

Current government reforms are transforming British public services. Instead of both financing and providing services, the state is becoming primarily a purchaser, with state provision being replaced by independent providers competing with one another in internal or quasi-markets. The method of finance is also changing. In some cases a centralised state agency continues to act as the principal purchaser. In others an earmarked budget or voucher is given directly to potential users, or to agents acting on their behalf, who then allocate the budget between competing providers.

The changes

Nowhere is this more apparent than in what we may soon have to stop calling the welfare state. In welfare areas such as education, health care, community care and housing, monopolistic state bureaucracies that both finance and provide the services concerned are disappearing. Health authorities now contract with semi-independent trusts to provide health care. In a parallel and potentially competitive development, some large general practitioner practices have 'fundholding' budgets so that they can purchase hospital care on behalf of their patients from the same provider.

Following the pattern set out in the White Paper *Caring for People*, local authority social services departments are increasingly purchasing community care services from private or voluntary agencies, while reducing their own provision. In some authorities 'care managers' are being introduced who, rather like general practitioner fund-holders, hold budgets on behalf of their clients from which they purchase community care for their clients.

Changes in school education include provisions for opting out, open enrolment, formula funding, and the local management of schools (LMS). Under the opting out provisons, schools

*This article is based on some of the material in Le Grand, J. and Bartlett, W. (eds) (1993), *Quasi-Markets and Social Policy*, Macmillan.

can choose whether to be funded by their local education authority or by the central government. Under open enrolment, parents can choose within certain limits the school to which they send their child. Under formula funding, the amount of resources a school opted out or not receives depends in large part on the number of pupils it can attract. Both opted out and LMS schools have been given control over the internal allocation of their resources, becoming in effect semi-independent providers. Together these reforms amount to a form of 'voucher' system, with resources no longer being primarily allocated to schools by a local bureaucracy, but by the choices of parents.

Council tenants are now able to choose their landlords from between competing suppliers. However, transfers of this kind have not been significant in practice. Instead, there has been a wave of interest among local authorities in voluntarily divesting themselves of their housing stock, generally to a specially created housing association, akin to a management buy-out of a monopoly supplier. Even more significant from the quasi-market perspective is the gradual but accelerating phenomenon of the expansion of the housing association movement to supplant local authorities as the main providers of social housing; while the role of the state as a funder is shifting from general 'bricks and mortar' subsidies to individual means-tested subsidy in the form of housing benefit. Again, this can be likened to a voucher; indeed its portability extends into the private rented sector.

Quasi-markets in the welfare state

All these developments thus involve the introduction of quasi-markets into the welfare state. They are 'markets' because they replace monopolistic state providers with competitive independent ones. They are 'quasi' because they differ from conventional markets in a number of key ways. The differences are on both the supply and the demand sides. On the supply side, as with conventional markets, there is competition between productive enterprises or service suppliers. Thus in all the schemes described there are independent institutions (schools, universities, hospitals, residential homes, housing associations, private landlords) competing for customers. However, in contrast to conventional markets, these organisations are not necessarily out to maximise their profits; nor are they necessarily privately owned. Precisely what such enterprises will maximise, or can be expected to maximise, is unclear, as is their ownership structure.

On the demand side, consumer purchasing power is not expressed in money terms. Instead it takes the form of an earmarked budget or 'voucher' confined to the purchase of a specific service. Also on the demand side, in some of the areas concerned such as health and social services, the immediate consumer is not the one who exercises the choices concerning purchasing decisions; instead those choices are delegated to a third party (a care manager, a general practitioner, or a health authority).

These welfare quasi-markets thus differ from conventional markets in one or more of three ways: not-for-profit organisations competing for public contracts, sometimes in competition with for-profit organisations; consumer purchasing power in the form of vouchers rather than cash; and, in some cases, using agents instead of operating by themselves.

Now advocates of markets or quasi-markets usually support them on the grounds that they promote efficiency, improve responsiveness and accountability and expand the range of opportunities and choices open to users. Critics argue that they may have such effects under favourable circumstances but that those favourable circumstances rarely arise in the welfare area. Also they point out that markets generally have other, undesirable, qualities, notably increased inequalities; that the introduction of a 'commercial' culture may seriously damage the relationship between professionals and their clients; and finally, that administration and other transaction costs may offset any cost reductions due to competitive pressures.

The reforms will take time to work their way through and it is too early to say whether the supporters or the critics will be proved right. However, there is an alternative approach to judging the likely outcomes of these changes. This is to specify the conditions that must be satisfied if quasi-markets in welfare are to achieve their ends without adverse consequences. There are five key conditions. First, the market structure must be *competitive* on both sides, with many providers and purchasers.

Competition is the engine of efficiency; if dissatisfied purchasers cannot take their business elsewhere, or if providers are at the mercy of monopolistic purchasers, incentives for efficiency or responsiveness are reduced, and providers are driven into other activities.

Second, both sides need access to cheap, accurate *information*, particularly concerning costs and quality. Providers must be able to cost their activities so as to be able to price them appropriately. Purchasers must be able to monitor the quality of the service they are purchasing, so as to limit the opportunity for providers to reduce costs by surreptitiously lowering quality.

Third, *transactions costs* – the costs of running a market – must be low. If the market requires substantial administrative resources, then this may offset any efficiency gains that might arise from its operations.

The fourth condition concerns *motivation*. Providers must be motivated at least in part by financial considerations. If they are not, if they are motivated largely by a sense of public duty, for instance, they will not respond appropriately to market signals. It makes little sense introducing a market to create profitable opportunities, if the participants in the market are not interested in making profits. It is for purchasers to promote the public interest; more specifically, their concern must be to further the interests of users to the greatest extent possible, given their resources.

Finally, there must be restricted opportunities for adverse selection or *cream-skimming*. Neither purchasers nor providers should be able to discriminate against the expensive or the troublesome 'user': the chronically ill patient, the incontinent, confused elderly person, the disruptive child from a deprived background. If either purchasers or providers can discriminate in favour of the relatively healthy, the competent and the easily educable, that is, if they can skim off the 'cream', then welfare services will not reach those who need them most.

It is not yet possible to say definitively whether these conditions are being fulfilled in practice. However, preliminary studies of several of the services concerned at the University of Bristol, the London School of Economics and elsewhere provide some disturbing signs. In the case of health authorities, the typical market structure, far from being competitive, is often closer to a bilateral monopoly, with a single purchaser and at best a few providers. Also the purchasers are heavily dependent on the providers for information; and they have few mechanisms for monitoring quality. In community care, the quasi-market is more competitive on the provider side, but as with health care, there are substantial information gaps. In response to this, purchasers often prefer to contract with voluntary organisations, whose non-profit motivation makes them less likely to exploit their informational advantage and to engage in cream-skimming. However, precisely because such organisations are not profit-maximisers, they lack the incentive to be cost-minimisers; hence any gains due to their reluctance to exploit their monopolistic position may be offset by a reduction in efficiency due to the absence of incentives for cost-minimisation.

The situation with respect to general practitioner fund-holding and education is rather different. In the case of education, the market structure does seem to be broadly competitive on both sides – although entry and exit into the market is limited. Also, the information gap is less than in other areas – although it still exists. Moreover, there do appear to be signs of some, surprisingly rapid, changes in behaviour in the direction that theory would predict, with some parents exercising their opportunities for choice and schools being motivated to make financial surpluses. However there also appear to be preliminary signs of cream-skimming, with schools setting up formal, or more commonly informal, means of selection.

General practioner fund-holding also appears to have considerable potential for improving efficiency. The quasi-market is competitive on both sides. Even more importantly, general practitioners have access to the best possible information concerning the quality of care: they can assess a patient's health before he or she goes into hospital and they can assess it when he or she comes out. On the negative side, the transaction costs to providers of negotiating with large numbers of fund-holders is high. And there is an obvious danger of cream-skimming by fund-holders in their selection of patients, although as yet there is little sign of this actually happening.

The quasi-market reforms are in their infancy and we cannot

yet assess their long-term consequences. However, we have seen that it is possible to combine theoretical considerations with some of the evidence that is now beginning to emerge on the process of implementation to make some preliminary assessments – or at least to point to areas where there might be possible sources of concern. It is perhaps over-simplistic, but we could summarise the argument so far by saying the health authority and social services reforms do not seem to hold out much prospect of efficiency gains, but may not have much adverse impact on equity either; whereas the education and general practitioner fund-holding reforms seem to hold out the prospects of real improvements in efficiency, responsiveness and choice, but may have a detrimental effect on equity.

Implications for social work education and training

There are a number of implications from all this for social work training. First, the development of care management, especially if accompanied by the devolution of budgets to care managers, means that social workers will have to be trained to act not so much as advocates for their clients, but as needs assessors and rationing agents. Second, budget holding will also require financial management skills. Third, social workers will need to develop the skills necessary for assessing the quality of providers, so as to reduce the possibility of providers engaging in opportunistic behaviour.

Fourth, and perhaps most important of all, there has to be a shift of training culture. Many of the people attracted into social work are intrinsically hostile to the idea of markets and, more generally, what they perceive as market ideology. But markets in general and quasi-markets in particular can be viewed simply as one of a set of possible mechanisms that can be used to achieve policy aims in the area of community care. As such, they have their problems; but so do other mechanisms, such as top-down hierarchical management systems or decentralised patch systems. What is needed is for social workers to obtain a balanced view of the relative merits and deficiencies of quasi-markets in welfare, as compared with other systems. In that way, they will be better placed to work in a quasi-market environment, taking advantage of the strengths of quasi-market systems and trying to rectify their weaknesses.

Educating for contracting and purchasing

BOB ANDERSON

Introduction

I have spent most of my working life as a teacher of social work. For the past five years, my job has involved me deeply in the new 'contract culture' and I can claim to have developed a fair degree of expertise in this. Inevitably, therefore, I find myself taking a rather personal approach in discussing the relationship between the two.

My approach is rather subjective and impressionistic but this is because it is about living and working successfully in an environment dominated by the market. However the conclusions I come to are similar to those of Julian Le Grand in the preceeding chapter. If he arrives at his conclusions from a theoretical starting point and I reach mine from an essentially practical starting point, this suggests these conclusions may have some validity.

Getting beyond the debate about values

The issue of social work values, and fears that they are incompatible with and threatened by the 'quasi-market', is attracting considerable attention. It may be heresy to set aside debate upon values and even more heretical to say that I've never been wholly sure of what is meant by social work values. Peter Beresford suggests a distillation down to concern for "the rights and needs and values of service users" in his discussion elsewhere in this book, which seems to me a valid summary. And if we accept this, where is the problem? It still guides you if you are a purchaser, driving the hardest bargain you can with a provider to get the best service you can for the price. It even guides you as a provider: every time I look at a contract proposed from one of our groups, I have to ask if this offers a fair deal for older people. Maybe that is what distinguishes a principled from an unprincipled provider – and one of the jobs for purchasers is to weed out unprincipled providers.

That isn't to say there are no moral dilemmas: of course there are – but that's a feature of life, not a feature of social work. Maybe these dilemmas become clearer to see, and therefore easier to resolve, within the new 'market'. The job of the purchaser is to maximise services for clients: if that means that the local authority home closes because the private alternative is more efficient, so be it: the duty of the social services department is to provide services for clients, not jobs for its staff. The duty of Age Concern is to promote the welfare of older people: if they can do it by employing me, so be it. If I outlive my usefulness, and the money can be better used in other ways, it is the clear duty of the executive committee to replace me. I may not like it, I may complain, I may suffer. I hope they will do it humanely and with consideration – that's all part of the value system. The bottom line, though, is that the interests of the beneficiaries in the case of Age Concern, the clients in the case of the social services department, must come first.

What needs to change

Let me turn to the other things apart from values which require attention if social workers are to operate in this new world.

First, I think there needs to be a major shift in the culture, the preconceptions, the attitudes of social work. Julian Le Grand asks that social workers "obtain a balanced view ... of quasi-markets". More than that, social workers need to accept that this is the environment in which they will be working, probably for most of their lives. I do not say we shouldn't question our working environment – whatever that environment is – but we also have to live with it. To sum up the change which is taking place: I spent my career training people to work in welfare agencies; now people are being trained to work in the 'care industry'.

The term may be disagreeable but it has come into circulation and I think it will be around for a long time. Within Age Concern it is now in use in debates about the future of the movement; I didn't flinch when a colleague on secondment to me from a commercial concern referred to his 'industry' and my 'industry'. I listened recently to a radio programme in which economists were discussing the contribution of the care industry to mopping up the European pool of low-skilled unemployed workers. My heart says I don't want to be part of the care industry; my head tells me that I am.

Social work has generally been developed with a vaguely liberal-to-left-wing ideology. The evolution of social services has been taught very much within the framework of a whig interpretation of history: of steady progress and improvement towards some ideal but ill-defined social democratic goal. Social work specifically has been intimately bound up with public-sector services, by far the major employers of social workers and now by far the most significant partners with the colleges in training. In selecting students, we have often favoured those – maybe in our own mould – who have rejected 'commercial pressures' in favour of 'helping people'. We have often, indeed usually, seen the concept of profit as incompatible with serving people. Now we find that we are having to accept a marriage of the two: we are having to face the prospect of working with care agencies run for profit. We find that we need to produce social workers who, whether as purchasers or providers, can combine commercial skills with care. In short, we are having to re-orient our thinking about how care is delivered.

Second, there needs to be significant expansion of knowledge and understanding within the social work profession. For example, very few of the social services department staff I come across, mostly middle to senior manager level, have much grasp of contract law. I've lost count of the times I've had to point out that the local authority service level agreement is an enforceable contract, or to explain to health authority staff why their internal contracts differ from those with outside agencies. Then there is the whole question of types of contract, their uses, the advantages and disadvantages. Block contract, cost-plus volume contract, spot contract: even at the most basic level, the social worker needs to know the framework within which he or she is working. There's a worrying ignorance also of voluntary organisations: of charity law, of the over-riding importance of a charity's objectives or the roles of trustees, of the agenda to which voluntary organisations work, and how they are managed. And of course future teaching about the voluntary sector will need to take account of the impact of the changes themselves. I think most of the existing textbooks will be obsolete in a few years time.

Then there is the understanding of finance. Social work has always seen money as a rather nasty topic which shouldn't be mentioned in polite company. It was legitimate to mention it in broad terms in social policy, or specifically in relation to welfare rights, but that was all. Once upon a time convincing my colleagues that working with poor clients was as legitimate a subject for study as working with mental health service users or old people presented difficulties. Now money is moving centre-stage – and a good thing too.

The phrase 'within available resources' isn't just a cautious political escape clause: it means something, and it brings us up sharp against reality. Purchasers and providers alike will no longer be able to carry blissfully on without worrying about the bill. They will need to understand costings, cost centres, unit costs and their relationship to volume, the difference between cost and price, the legitimacy of profit, the significance of cash-flow: every single one of these terms has emerged as a significant factor in the contract negotions in which I have been involved. This is not a matter of accountancy theory, but about the practicalities of making contracts work and getting viable, effective, sustainable services delivered.

These areas of knowledge, and especially the last, run into the third and final area I wish to mention: skills. One of the most obviously necessary skills in contracting is the skill of negotia-tion: sound contracts are the end-product of negotiation. It is also one of the skills most conspicuously lacking. So far, many social services departments have seen contracting as a matter of stating their terms to providers on a take-it-or-leave-it basis; they have often been able to do this, in residential care particularly, because they are shopping in a buyer's market. I suspect this will change when the market has shaken out, and over-provision is not a feature: then providers will be able to negotiate from a much stronger position.

An equally important skill, in urgent need of development, relates to defining, specifying and measuring quality. Most of us think we know good day care, for example, when we see it: but what makes it good, how can we set down what we feel, how can we measure one centre against another in any objective way? So far contracts are tending to rely on two features: evidence of user satisfaction, which is important but may be flawed – users may be happy in their day centre, but it may not be doing exactly the job expected of it and their experience and information may be limited; or measurements of input – proportion of qualified staff, training programmes, safety measures, equal opportunities policies and the like. But again that may not be enough: some well-resourced day care is unsatisfactory, some apparently amateurish day care produces excellent results. Most people would say we should be specifying and measuring outcomes, and many people are trying to do this. But my experience suggests that in this area, more than any other, purchasers, providers and users have to learn together.

In conclusion, purchasing and contracting is probably the best thing that has happened to social work in my lifetime. It puts social work back where it always should have been: arranging, as efficiently as possible, services to meet clients' needs. Like child protection, it provides a clear functional purpose for a profession which has often tended to drift, trying to discover its destiny. It pulls us back from the further shores of social engineering or personal therapy, and it makes us engage in practical tasks such as making the most efficient use of available resources, which we have often tried to evade.

Social work as a public health activity: collaboration and conflict in the new environment

MARIA DUGGAN

Introduction

The gulf between the health and social care sectors which has bedevilled the best efforts of both health and social care practitioners to plan and deliver 'seamless services' to people in the community seems as deep now as it has ever been. Indeed cost shunting between local authorities and demarcation disputes between local agencies have been an increasing feature of the community care landscape since the enactment of the legislation and there is every sign that these are going to continue.

This is an alarming and unexpected scenario if consideration is given to the clear intention of the National Health Service and Community Care Act and accompanying guidance, with their exhortations to promote and develop partnerships between all local agencies involved in the delivery of community care. It is even more surprising if we consider the rapidly evolving primary care arena which is bringing professionals within the various disiplines into new relationships with each other and where the interface between health needs and social care needs is in itself an increasingly important site for intervention and co-operation.

These developments appear at first glance to be in conflict with each other. At best, this conflict exemplifies that glaring gap between government rhetoric and the underfunded reality of life on the ground. At worst it has been seen by some as a deliberate attempt by government to obscure the destruction of both the National Health Service and social welfare provision in this country behind a smoke screen of unattainable targets and the creation of ineffective "healthy alliances" (Pollock, 1994/5).

Pressures and problems

There is indeed cause for great concern about this gap. Recent research indicates that a range of factors threatens to undermine the community care reforms. It is suggested that these pressures stem as much from changes in the National Health Service which are placing "burdens upon the community care reforms that they were never meant to sustain" (Wistow, 1995) as from underfunding per se. Among these changes are the shifting boundaries between the acute and community health care sectors and the increasing power of primary care led purchasing to shift and reconfigure the pattern of services across the board.

Clearly these fundamental changes stem in part from the ambitious programme of reform which has so fundamentally transformed the National Health Service since the mid 1970s. However a range of other factors needs to be taken into account. These include the influence of developments in medical technology, improved pharmacology and anaesthesia and minimally invasive surgery. These developments, taken together with cost improvement pressures to reduce lengths of stay and to increase rates of day surgery, create a range of situations that have to be managed outside of the traditional hospital setting within the broadening arena of extended primary care.

In the context of *Caring for People*, these trends are reinforced by the volume of elderly patients who use acute beds. Forty seven per cent of all acute beds in 1992-93 can be attributed to elderly users. Yet similar trends to those noted above are evident in geriatric services, with available beds down over a fifth since 1989. This process is challenging our traditional models of conceptualising and delivering health care services. It is also creating a profoundly different culture within which health and welfare services are obliged to perform. The scale and scope of these changes have in effect imposed a new dimension on the context within which care in the community is having to operate.

The implications for social work and social services

The implications of this for departments of social services, voluntary agencies and carers are immensely significant. Massive changes are taking place within social care roles and functions and these are experienced on either side of the purchaser/provider split. New thresholds are being determined daily, particularly in relation to the boundary between health and social care, frailty and infirmity, clinical as opposed to non-clinical needs and the distinction between needs and wants. New territory is being opened up within which social care professionals must operate. The contours of this territory are bounded by functions such as the provision of personal and bodily care and bathing services, planned programmes of rehabilitative home care and the negotiating of service level agreements with providers. Changes such as these with their undoubted threats also bring with them possibilities and opportunities for enhancing the role of social care professionals, including social workers, and of adapting both role and function to meet the demands of the new environment.

Consider the following statement by the district manager of a social services department elders team:

"We have major problems in agreeing a division of labour between social services employees and nurses. Whose responsibility is it to perform certain caring tasks like giving eye drops after cataract operations, administering pessaries? District nurses will only bathe patients at home if they have what is considered to be a full medical condition. Otherwise they expect the home helps to do it. Problems also exist in relation to discharge from hospital and continuing care. We have very real difficulties in palliative care. Health says that they are contracted to do hospice care only, not community care. Social services is left with the cost of providing an intensive care package with very little input from general practitioners or nurses" (Duggan, 1995).

This statement clearly reflects the range of threats being imposed upon local authority departments of social services by the reconfigured National Health Service landscape. It reflects also the sense of despair of one social work manager. The sentiments will be familiar to all practitioners and have led to the continuing debate about the desirability of merging health and social care planning functions and budgets, and the growing view that responsibility for purchasing health care should be transferred to the local authorities. Such sentiments have frequently determined a response from within the social work profession which is defensive and nostalgic for what is now perceived as a lost golden age of social work, "defenders of the old guard rather than the vanguard of the new order" (Harvey and Philpot, 1993). Such nostalgia correctly identifies the structural and financial pressures on the district manager quoted above and many others, but has so far failed to provide adequate explanations as to why the services outlined should not be provided through social care. Indeed, as primary care develops and extends its boundaries, social work in particular could have a major role to play in shaping the provision of services which can attend holistically to individual needs, and which are not dominated by medical ideologies and practices. Unless these opportunities are grasped, the unique perspective of social work may be marginal within the new primary care environment.

These challenges have faced social work before. Over fifteen years ago, Colin Brewer and June Lait asked the question "Can social work survive?" (Brewer and Lait, 1980). Although the anti-social work arguments of this work, which predicted the end of the profession, have been proven to be wrong, the same question must now be asked again but for different reasons. These reasons include the profound impact that care management is having on the practice of social work, as well as the realignment of health and social care within primary care. Evidence of the value of the former is beginning to emerge (Challis, 1993). It will be necessary in the near future to map the impact of the latter changes on the practice of social work.

Arguably, the results of such an exercise will be illuminating and surprising. Among the opportunities which are potentially available to social work professionals are the development of an enhanced knowledge base to take account of both National Health Service and social services history, culture and structure; and the development of an understanding of the multiple causes and cures of ill health, to understand what is necessary for rehabilitation and maintenance of people with long-term limiting illnesses and impairments, and the management of care of people with terminal illnesses. All of these activities have been notoriously under-developed within the social work repertoire until now.

Add to these the development of enhanced negotiation and management skills and of skills in quantative and qualitative research, which will be increasingly required as purchasing is led from within primary care and services are purchased and provided to meet the assessed needs of individuals and populations; and the evolution of modern social work is complete. It can be situated very broadly within an arena that is increasingly understood as the "new public health" (Public Health Alliance, 1988) and which is essentially concerned with the causes of ill health and with problems of equity and social justice. The World Health Organisation defines public health as "the science and art of preventing disease, prolonging life and promoting health through the organised efforts of society". Increasingly, the new public health is perceived as a non-medical, multi-sectoral speciality. The social work perspective has much to contribute to it.

Whether or not this new model needs to co-exist with or to replace the traditional form of social work is open to debate. There may be some lessons to be learned from the continuing evaluation of care management, which has been seen variously as an evolved, specialist or debased social work role. The polarisation of social work and care management which is discernible in the literature is not necessarily an accurate reflection of reality. Olive Stevenson for one suggests that care management, properly practised, ought to contain two essential aspects, counselling and social care planning (Stevenson, 1993). Both of these were identified by the Barclay Report (1982) as being the essential components of social work.

The implications for social work education

So what might this all mean for social work education? Clearly, if the basic argument is accepted, there is a requirement for change within social work training curricula to embrace the health service and other dimensions outlined above. More radically, there is a need to open up social work education and to locate the function and practice of social work within the new environment. This will require new attitudes towards joint training and education with all of the professionals involved in primary care as a start. This must embrace the perspectives of carers and service users, and opportunities for developing partnership approaches to training involving these groups need to be developed as a matter of urgency. In addition, academic departments of social work need to consider the implications and strategies for joint training with general practitioners and community nurses, public health professionals, professions auxiliary to medicine and even with acute medical staff. The profession needs to determine what is core and what is at the interface and ensure that learning from other perspectives is built in from the start: the rewards could be immense.

Seamless care requires seamless policy and willing and creative interactions from the many professionals and carers who purchase and provide community care. These seams must, in the words of Gerald Wistow, be "joined at the design stage and not patched together during the process of implementation". The evolution in primary care provides a new point of departure for the development of true seamlessness, based on an understanding of what is required to create and maintain the conditions for optimal social health. This process of joining and merging perspectives needs to begin with education. Social work education has a major contribution to play. It needs to seize the challenge and move forward with it.

Networking and social work education

STEVE TREVILLION

Introduction

We often associate community care with key issues such as the implications of the purchaser/provider split and the end of generic social work. But we do not pay as much attention to its impact on what used to be called 'social work methods'. The purpose of the paper is to draw attention to the central role which is likely to be occupied by the new method of networking in the emerging community care curriculum.

More specifically my intention is:

1. to outline the background to the development of networking as a key community care practice

2. to discuss some of the implications for social work education of a research and development project on networking undertaken by myself and a team from the then West London Institute (now Brunel University College) in the London Borough of Hounslow

3. to discuss the way in which we have sought to address networking in the form and content of the curriculum.

Networking and social work

If there are three words which sum up contemporary social work preoccupations they are 'partnership', 'empowerment' and 'community'. Networking is intimately connected with all three. In a sense, it forges a link between all three because it bases itself on the idea of a web of reciprocal relationships (Jordan, 1990) underpinning social work practice.

Networking is:

"all those activities which enable separate individuals, groups or organisations to join with one another in social networks which enhance communication and/or active co-operation and create new opportunities for choice and empowerment for at least some if not all of those taking part" (Trevillion, 1992).

But networking has not simply emerged fully formed in the context of contemporary debates about welfare. Although it is, as I will argue, a potentially revolutionary approach to social work, it can also paradoxically claim to be part of the mainstream of social work theory; a key reference point being the 1980s debate about community social work.

One major link between networking and community social work is, for example, the concept of the interwoven social support network developed in the 1970s and early 1980s (Bayley, 1973; Garbarino, 1983). There are also connections between networking and more recent movements: applied social network analysis (Seed, 1990), feminist (Dominelli and McLeod, 1989) and anti-racist social work (Dominelli, 1988) have all contributed to the formation of core knowledge, values and skills, as have allied developments in community work (for example Henderson and Thomas, 1987).

Networking and the 'soft revolution'

What has drawn all these different strands together is the impact of community care on the whole way in which we think about professional roles and tasks. It is now taken for granted that an ability to cross professional boundaries, take account of multiple perspectives and work flexibly and creatively with others will become increasingly vital if the community care reforms are to succeed in their stated aims (Laming, 1989).

Community care has plunged us into a world in which the old either/or language of statutory versus voluntary, public versus private, social work versus health, providers versus consumers of services is no longer up to the task of describing what is going on in the increasingly fluid and rapidly changing welfare environment. To give just one example of particular relevance for networking: in the days of community social work, with one or two notable exceptions there was still an assumption that social workers would be based in generic Seebohm style teams with other social workers, even if this team was based in a particular locality or 'patch', as favoured by Hadley and his supporters (Barclay, 1982). But with the coming of new developments in primary care and community care, the whole concept of 'teams' and 'teamwork' has become very unclear (Jones, 1992). We can no longer take for granted that every 'team' to which social workers belong will have a shared office or a shared professional identity, let alone a distinct territory, as in the days of patch.

As the debate about teams becomes a debate about networks of collaboration – patterns of roles, relationships, communication and mutual understanding (Hutchinson and Gordon, 1992) linking all the diverse groups associated with community care, we have to find a new softer, more malleable kind of language to describe these new working relationships – a language of process rather than structure, a language of mediation and permeability rather than one of rigid boundaries and territorial defensiveness. It is this fact which has more than anything else pulled together a number of previously disparate practices to form our contemporary notion of networking.

It is easy to think of collaboration as the acceptable face of community care, that aspect of it which is comfortable and reassuring in comparison with the often harsh free market rhetoric associated with the purchase/provider split. But as I have indicated collaboration is in many ways as subversive of traditional practices and beliefs as competition.

However you look at it, community care is breaking down organisational structures and forcing a radical re-think about the whole nature of professional role and identity in relation to 'the community'. Networking is one of the products of this radical review. Through networking, social work is entering a postmodern phase of its development. One feature of the 'soft revolution' associated with the collaborative imperative is that social work will be much less concerned with providing a particular welfare service than with constantly breaking down and re-inventing welfare in collaboration with service users, carers and other professionals in an unpredictable post-welfare state world.

In practical terms this means social work will be concerned with building social fields capable of generating choice and empowerment in contexts of conflict and scarcity.

Researching the core competences in networking

Any social worker seeking to develop the kind of collaborative social fields which I have described will have to possess certain skills, grounded on a particular knowledge base and a coherent set of values. In other words, it seems likely that there are competencies in networking which will become increasingly important to anyone practising social work.

But what are these networking competencies?

To find out, a team from the West London Institute led by Peter Beresford and myself undertook a project on collaboration and collaborative skills in Hounslow from 1992-93, working closely with both the health authority and the social services department. We were sponsored by the Central Council for Education and Training in Social Work as part of its programme of research and development designed to "integrate community care into the Post Qualifying (PQ) framework" (CCETSW, 1990).* One of the collaborative practices we explored was networking.

Professionals were recruited to the research from both the local authority social services department and from the health authority on the basis of their interest and involvement in community care work in general and networking in particular. Service users and carers from the same geographical area were invited to participate on a similar basis, that is their experience of community care and their interest in contributing to the development by professionals of relevant skills.

The research model could be described as that of two streams converging into a final synthesis. One stream consisted of work with service users and carers based on group discussions. The other stream consisted of work with professionals based on diaries and group discussions. The final synthesis was accomplished in a workshop.

Research outcomes

The final workshop attended by all those involved in the project led us to focus our attention on six key areas of competency identified as critical by professionals, that is social workers and nurses, managers and practitioners, carers and service users

---

* The sections of this paper which describe this research project are based on a much fuller account in Beresford, P. and Trevillion, S. (1995) *Developing Skills for Community Care: A Collaborative Approach*, Arena.

alike. All of these involved networking.

Developing communication networks – this involved a wide range of skills from simply knowing how to listen to and talk to people, through to strategic thinking around patterns of communication and the resolution of communication problems.

Developing inter-personal relationships – from building trust and support to handling anxiety and conflict.

Shifting the balance of power in community care networks – from simply being prepared to 'stick up' for service users, through to helping non-professionals such as service users and carers or quasi-professionals such as home helps to develop professional skills in chairing meetings, minute taking and so on.

Assessing and planning with community care networks – from the analysis of patterns of need through to the ability to access resources in new and imaginative ways.

Developing network identity and purpose – involving the ability to discover common purpose in the middle of complexity and difference and to work to objectives with a complex range of different partners.

Reviewing the progress of initiatives with community care networks – involving the ability to analyse and to be self critical along with the ability to enable others to develop these same abilities.

Building on the research outcomes we were able to define not only broad areas of competency but underlying values, knowledge and skills which in many ways are characteristic of collaborative work as a whole, but also have a particular significance for those actively working to develop community care networks of various kinds.

The core values

The first striking feature about the values associated with networking is the continuity with the past. Whilst networking was a relatively new area of activity for most of the professionals involved in the project, it appeared to have its roots in some familiar professional principles.

The social workers involved in the project adhered to the traditional precepts of 'respect for persons' and 'acceptance' and showed they were as relevant for networking as they were for social casework. The nurses involved in the project adhered to the 'whole person' philosphy of nursing, itself based on the holistic view of health and therefore the holistic nature of the work of the health professional. But there is also something distinctive about the 'networking belief system'.

There is a very strong emphasis upon :

• honesty and openness, a willingness to learn from others

• a commitment to flexibility, informality and creativity

• a commitment to sharing power vis a vis service users, carers and other professionals.

The core knowledge base

The necessarily wide ranging kinds of interventions associated with networking make it difficult to identify a clearly bounded and exclusive body of knowledge associated with it. However, the following appear to be essential elements of the knowledge base:

• the characteristics of social networks and an ability to apply this knowledge to community care with a particular emphasis upon all aspects of social support

• concepts of power and authority and the ability to apply this knowledge to the analysis of how oppression manifests itself in social fields of various kinds, especially those involving professionals and non-professionals

• the ability to work with conflict and ambivalence, especially in relation to the process of negotiation

• the variety of organisational systems and cultures, together with an understanding of how these concepts can be applied to inter-agency and intra-agency work on the one hand, and work with organisations of service users and carers on the other

• an understanding of processes of communication, especially informal processes

• knowledge of 'action set theory' and its relevance to an understanding co-ordination and mobilisation in the special circumstances of community care.

The core skills

As with the core values, there is clear evidence from our research that some traditional methods of intervention continue to be relevant to networking for community care. Community development work, group work and counselling, together with a demonstrable ability to deploy these skills in appropriate combinations, all have their place in the networking repertoire. Moreover, skills in anti-discriminatory practice are as important to networking as to any other type of welfare work.

But there are also areas of skill much more specifically linked to networking:

- community brokerage, that is the process of helping to create and sustain purposeful links between separate individuals, groups or agencies – developing and sustaining patterns of communication and patterns of support

- mobilising people and resources, together with the skills required to ensure adequate co-ordination

- reflective critical ethnography, which is linked to an ability to empathise with more than one perspective and to think critically about all of them, including one's own

- strategies for opening up decision making processes through creative problem solving

- facilitating and chairing network meetings or conferences.

Developing the core competences in the Diploma in Social Work and beyond

While I would not go so far as to claim that this is an exhaustive list of all the values, areas of knowledge and skills required for competent networking, let alone collaborative work, in general I feel that together all these things could be described as the core competences for networking. In other words, achieving competence in networking for community care is likely to be directly related to the acquisition of these core competences.

I now move on to discuss how competences in networking can be developed within the broader context of preparing professional social workers for the challenge of collaboration in community care. A comprehensive answer to this question is beyond the scope of this discussion. But we need to acknowledge that it raises questions about the form as well as the content of the curriculum. I will look, briefly, at some of these, drawing where appropriate on the Hounslow research.

Multi-disciplinary education and training

All those who participated in the Hounslow project emphasised the need for dialogue with other professionals more than anything else. This suggests that much post-qualifying training in community care should be of a multi-disciplinary nature. But what about the Diploma in Social Work? Is a strong multi-disciplinary element going to strengthen or weaken professional identity? I would argue for multi-disciplinary education at Diploma in Social Work level, because the Hounslow project showed that working closely with other professionals could consolidate rather than undermine appropriate professional values, especially in relation to networking.

Learning opportunities

Can networking be taught in college or is it essentially a practical agency-based activity? In my view, networking is like any other part of the curriculum. Both college and agency can make a contribution, in that learning opportunities can be found or made in both contexts. What is different about networking, however, is that even agency and college working together may not be enough to deliver the curriculum. All students should also spend some time with other professionals, and this may mean spending time in another agency, not just another part of the placement or employing agency. At Post Qualifying level I would suggest that every module of study contains a college component, a practice component and a participant observation component in another professional setting. But again, what about the Diploma in Social Work? Here I think we should also be prepared to be flexible. Colleges with both health and social work departments might find new ways of co-operating with one another in this area.

Service user and carer involvement in professional education

Service user trainers and carer trainers should be given a much more central role at both Diploma in Social Work and Post Qualifying levels. Expertise in networking takes many different forms and service users and carers have a lot to say about what partnership in community care might involve and how social workers can be more sensitive and effective.

The structure of the curriculum

In year one of the Diploma in Social Work the need is for a major focus on collaboration and its implications for practice, and this should include a specific input on networking showing the range of its application to all client groups. In year two students need to be helped to link networking more specifically to community care, but also to deepen their understanding of its use with a wide range of different client groups.

Currently at Brunel University College, all year one students participate in a workshop on networking at the end of the year. Some students opt for a specialist course in networking and care management in year two. In the future, I would like us to develop a multi-disciplinary module at Diploma in Social Work level, perhaps in year two. We have also just set up a part-time masters course in community care with a major emphasis on collaboration in which skills in networking will be interwoven with skills in involvement.

Delivering the curriculum – teaching and learning strategies

The curriculum could be delivered and assessed in a range of different ways. I have personally found workshops very useful, particularly at the introductory stage. We currently run a one-day workshop in which first year students are asked to explore key issues through the use of a network sculpt. This experiential approach has generated some very interesting learning.

As a result of the workshop last summer students identified the following issues, which I quote verbatim:

"Be clear about your role and about the roles of others,

maintain good communication and aim to work in collaboration"

"An initial assessment that recognises the emotional and practical needs of the family and which avoids bombarding the family just with resources"

"Be sensitive to family relationships"

"Identify the key people and encourage them to communicate their own needs to each other (and professionals)"

"Liaise with professionals concerned to mobilise appropriate resources".

In my view these comments demonstrate significant learning about many of the key issues surrounding community care, that is communication difficulties, lack of support, role confusion, oppressive relationships, scarce resources and ineffective working arrangements. Moreover the sculpt gave these students the opportunity to experiment with ways of addressing these problems.

Recently, second year students themselves chose to use a sculpt to analyse a particular situation involving problems of communication between a medical 'team' and a social worker. They used it very creatively. It is this kind of initiative which tends to confirm my belief in the value of sculpts, because they are especially well suited to the exploration of relationships in spatial terms.

Conclusion

I have tried to locate networking in the context both of the traditions of social work and the specific challenge posed to practice by the community care revolution. I have also tried to show how the results of a development project have influenced our thinking at Brunel University College about ways of incorporating networking within both the Diploma in Social Work and the Post Qualifying curricula.

I believe that although networking is deeply rooted in the social work tradition, it also represents part of a 'paradigm shift' brought about by the new emphasis on collaboration in the delivery of community care. What needs to be acknowledged, of course, is that before we can help our students to come to terms with what I have called the 'soft revolution', we have to think our way through it ourselves.

The way forward

DENISE PLATT

Before considering the 'way forward' I want to look first at the past and the present.

Care in the community policies reflect a clear intention to provide services on an entirely different basis from before – to help people to live within their own communities, to help them to retain their independence, to provide them with relevant support tailored to their particular circumstances, and to help them to retain as much choice and control as possible over their own lives.

Both the National Health Service and Community Care Act and the Children Act, as with other legislation to affect local government, require the local authority to assume a strategic planning role in the community. The expectation is that we should 'enable' services to develop rather than 'provide' them all ourselves. Departments are required to work alongside other agencies who provide care, and the respective responsibilities should be clearly identified.

Both pieces of legislation require changes in the culture of social services organisations and the way we deliver services. The emphasis is on individual needs and packages of care, provison of information about services, open decision making that is capable of challenge through complaints procedures, provision of choice, user-led rather than supply-led services and targeting resources to people most in need. Alongside this is a shift in public expectations and the rise of consumerism, putting services under pressure and scrutiny.

The challenge for staff in moving to needs-led assessments for services is more difficult than anticipated. We are so used to putting together packages of the services we have, rather than listening to the articulation of individual need and giving choice.

The concept of the enabling authority applies across all public sector services – the health service, local government and services within local government. The enabling authority is responsible for identifying the needs of the population it serves, publishing plans for the provision of services in its area, deciding objectives and priorities and securing the delivery of services by use of its purchasing and contracting role as well as, in certain circumstances, acting as the direct provider. Overall, it is responsible for ensuring that the services provided are of good quality and give value for money.

The enabling authority works alongside all sectors – independent and voluntary – in the development of the mixed economy of care and service. There are many areas of adult care services where the mixed economy is flourishing – housing association involvement in accommodation for people with special needs; much independent sector provision in residential care; and widespread voluntary sector involvement in service provision.

The statutory sector has an important role in stimulating other providers to respond to the needs that have been identified. This purchasing/commissioning function ensures that services are needs-led, are based upon the identification of needs for the local community, are responsive to local needs, that individual packages of care can be tailor-made to the needs of individual people and that in focusing on community needs and individual needs, better gender and culture sensitive services can be developed. Purchasing and its separation from provision is seen as a critical mechanism to achieve the transition from a service driven definition of needs to a needs driven definition of service, and a critical tool in the development of an enabling authority.

A social services director now has three roles – as the enabler and purchaser of social care services; as the direct provider of services; as the inspector and regulator of service provision.

New agenda

We are beginning to develop a collaborative agenda in community care and there is still much to do. The realisation of the mixed economy; the full implementation of care management systems; the move towards joint commissioning; refining needs analysis – these are strategic issues which all authorities are now having to address.

At the same time as we are being encouraged to work together to achieve this complex agenda, there are many tensions which appear to be driving us apart. The sharp differentiation of roles into purchaser or provider – both within and without

organisations – is a new concept in social care. Market mechanisms are increasing the number of organisations who have an
interest in social care across many service areas. Health, education and housing are critical partners. They are also subject to
change and reorganisaion. Many of the routine ways of working
together in the past are now challenged. We not only have to
cope with our own change, but that of everyone else as well. Just
knowing who people are is a problem and recognising their title
even more of a challenge.

There are many different organisational arrangements being
developed across social services departments; many departments
have had radical restructures. It is more important than ever to
have an understanding of what the structures are trying to
achieve. Nothing can be taken for granted by looking at the title
of a post.

Neither is it the case that the environment in which we are all
working supplies a stable background. Both local government
and the National Health Service are currently subject to further
major changes through both the local government review, the
regrouping of health authorities into larger purchasing agencies
and the scaling down of regional health authorities. And our
resources are ever changing.

The social care market is different from other markets. It is
not just an internal market, as in the National Health Service.
There are real competitors for social services in service delivery.
There are more sectors contributing and more organisations
which have been providing services for long periods of time.
Many people have difficulty in participating in this market and
have to be assisted. Many people who use the service can't shop
around. Many people who use services are involuntary users of
those services. And it is the case that the outcomes are difficult
to predict. The market is a managed market rather than a free
market.

The delivery of effective community care services relies on a
set of interdependent activities between agencies. Although there
are separate roles, responsibilities and functions, the effective
achievement of a co-ordinated service requires a network of
interdependent organisations across the sectors of social care –
public, private and voluntary. We need to find new ways of

working in collaboration to achieve this.

It is important in this atmosphere of change that we remember that what we are all aiming to achieve is better co-ordinated services, an improved assessment process and an improved experience for people who need support.

New skills

There are many new and changing roles in social services departments. At present most of these new roles are assumed by qualified social work staff, whether they be new 'commissioning', 'inspecting' or 'care management' roles. People with other training qualifications are moving into all of these roles, but the predominant profession is still social work. All are having to develop new skills – to grasp and put into practice the basic essentials of assessment, creating care packages, budgeting and to ensure the principles of choice and participation are carried out.

Commissioning staff are simultaneously expanding and developing services in the domiciliary care sector while other staff are reducing services in the residential sector. We have to develop new skills in enabling new markets to develop – and we need to appreciate the major impact of our decisions on providers.

Purchasers and care managers are having to develop new skills in identifying need, both of communities and of individuals, and to translate this analysis into a specification for service. Involving the user and carer is critical to this process, otherwise assessment will continue to be professionally led.

Purchasers need to develop the skills to support and encourage those organisations who are capable of delivering effective services and to be sensitive to the needs and vulnerability of those delivering services, avoiding 'macho' tactics and shows of strength.

Providers' roles are changing. In-house services are having to become more businesslike in their approach and have much to learn from the private sector in costing and marketing their services. The voluntary sector is learning how it will respond to service level agreements rather than grants. Working to service specifications, attempting to develop them with the user and the local authority/ health service purchasers are new and demanding requirements.

All are needing to develop skills and competence in :

- partnership – developing these across agencies, with users and carers and between purchasers

- encouraging participation – in identifying needs, deciding the most appropriate services, and to provide feedback on quality

- offering choice – choice of lifestyle, of how services are delivered and in day to day decisions in residential care which affect dignity and privacy

- responding to change – the ability to cope with change, personally as a worker and within services.

Social work

So where does this leave social workers and the values which underpin their work? Some of course may never work in statutory agencies in future; or if they do perhaps not for their whole career, or they will move between sectors more freely than at present. Traditional career paths will most certainly change. The social work task has never been under so much scrutiny. In 1993 the Association of Directors of Social Services held a media seminar to examine some of the adverse publicity surrounding social work and social services. We were told by a well-known leader writer that social services were "a minority service, serving minority clients, who are unpopular". The public and political view of people who use social services – single parents, juvenile offenders, mental health service users – has become less tolerant. What we have seen is a call for a change from supportive to punitive values.

We are asked whether we 'condone or condemn' juvenile offending. But it is not our function to make absolute judgments of this sort, to apportion blame to individuals. This does not mean that social services considers criminal activity in young people as acceptable, nor does it mean that the problems of the victims are thought to be less important.

Social workers stand in the middle of this debate. Because of their experience and understanding of the pressures on families they are likely to have more realistic expectations of what can or cannot be achieved. It is of course important for children to have a stable home background, to know the difference between right and wrong, to learn to be responsible citizens. But many families need help to get there, help to get back into education, to learn self discipline. The disagreement is about how this might be achieved, what is the place of rehabilitation and what responsibility does the community have to help.

But articulating this is unpopular and results in the work social workers are attempting to do with people to be publicly derided. Much of our work is an assessment of the risks which are present in the circumstances of children and families, people leaving psychiatric hospitals or elderly and frail people who wish to live in their own homes – risks which can sometimes go wrong and then the broader public may be unsympathetic.

Some of these views wash over into community care: reading some commentators you could be forgiven for thinking that social work is irrelevant to effective community care, or an optional extra. This is not my view. My own authority's experience has shown that very skilled social work is necessary in much assessment work – especially where the interests of carer and user conflict; where severely distressed people need skilful multi-disciplinary work; in ongoing care management, helping those with deteriorating physical conditions to make decisions about their future. Social work values and experience have been necessary inputs to developing informed service specifications and developing inspection standards.

We have had much debate about 'political correctness', especially regarding equal opportunities policies and race. I do not know what 'political correctness' means, given the amount of adverse political comment that is attracted by anyone accused of it. I am told it is 'fashionable thinking'. I have much sympathy with people who are critical of jargon. I have learnt interesting jargon from the National Health Service which serves to conceal the real meaning of the words. For example 'cost shunting' means somebody else pays, but it sounds a good business technique; and 'managed exit' means cutting a service. Explaining in plain language what we do is important. The 'political correctness' debate avoids discussion of the real issues of concern, and inhibits our capacity to address them.

Social workers work in a multi-racial environment. There is a shared heritage, but there are differences in our background, our origins and our experiences of day to day life in general. It is important that we recognise that different groups living in our communities have different experiences. If we do not, we ignore the influences which shape them as people, and we cannot respond to their proper social services needs adequately.

It is of concern to all of us that there are more Black than white people being sectioned under the Mental Health Act, or being placed inappropriately in residential care. My commisioning staff visited an independent home for older people and met a woman only recently placed there by her local authority qualified social worker. The woman could not speak English. None of the staff could speak her language and had to communicate by waving their arms. She only spoke her own language on the monthly visit of her son. This is not meeting someone's needs adequately; this is not dignity or respect. And she was not the only person they found in such circumstances.

We have to address these issues, and give social workers practical strategies for tackling them. It is irresponsible not to equip workers who are confronting these situations daily with the expertise to understand and to act.

We should not be defensive and abandon knowledge gained from experience in tackling social problems in local communities. We should not abandon values which underpin social work and which are ever present in the new legislation and its guidance.

What I needed as a director of social services were social workers with knowledge, skills and most importantly competences to carry out the tasks, who know and understand the legislative framework, who can operate effectively within new statutory requirements, who can understand and work within the new organisational arrangements and culture of social services, who can respond to change as it affects both their own role and tasks and the service they work in.

No small challenge for us all!

References

Barclay, P. (1982), *Social Workers: Their role and tasks*, National Institute for Social Work/Bedford Square Press.

Bayley, M. (1973), *Mental Handicap and Community Care: A study of mentally handicapped people in Sheffield*, Routledge and Kegan Paul.

Beresford, P. (1994), *Changing the Culture: Involving service users in social work education*, Paper 32:2, Central Council for Education and Training in Social Work.

Beresford, P. (1995), Community Care Funding Crisis Threatens the User Ideal, *Community Care*, 9-15 February.

Beresford, P. and Trevillion, S. (1995), *Developing Skills for Community Care: A collaborative approach*, Arena.

Bowis, J. (1994), Meeting of Department of Health National Users and Carers Group, 14 July.

Brewer, C. and Lait, J. (1980), *Can Social Work Survive?*, Temple Smith.

Butt, J. (1994), *Same Service or Equal Service?*, HMSO.

CCETSW (1990), *The Requirements for Post-qualifying Education and Training in the Personal Social Services*, Paper 31, Central Council for Education and Training in Social Work.

Challis, D. (1993), Care Management: Observations from a programme of research, *PSSRU Bulletin*, 9.

Community Care (1995), Academics Form New Committee, 20-26 July.

Dominelli, L. (1988), *Anti-Racist Social Work*, Macmillan.

Dominelli, L. and McLeod, E.(1989), *Feminist Social Work*, Macmillan.

Duggan, M. (1995), *Primary Health Care: A prognosis*, Institute of Public Policy Research.

European Commission (1994), *European Social Policy Options for the Union*, EC Directorate General for Employment.

Evans, M. and Pottage, D. (1994), *The Competent Workplace: The view from within*, National Institute for Social Work.

Family Welfare Association (1994), *The Future of Welfare*, RSA.

Garbarino, J. (1983), Social Support Networks: RX for the helping professions in Whittaker, J. and Garbarino, J.(eds) *Social Support Networks: Informal helping in the social services*, Aldine.

Harding, T. (1992), *Great Expectations... and Spending on the Social Services*, National Institute for Social Work.

Harding, T. and Beresford, P. (1996), *The Standards We Expect*, National Institute for Social Work.

Harvey, C. and Philpot, T. (1993), Embracing the Future, *Community Care*, 16 November.

Henderson, P. and Thomas D. (1987), *Skills in Neighbourhood Work*, Allen and Unwin.

Hill, M.(1993), *The Fulcrum of Welfare: A guide to the debate,* Joseph Rowntree Foundation.

Hutchinson, A. and Gordon, S. (1992), Primary Care Teamwork - Making it a reality, *Journal of Interprofessional Care,* vol.6, no.1.

Hutton, W. (1995), *The State We Are In,* Jonathan Cape.

Jones, C. (1994/5), CCETSW in Shambles, *Community Care,* 22 December - 5 January.

Jones, R. (1992), Teamwork in Primary Care: How much do we know about it? *Journal of Interprofessional Care,* vol.6, no.1.

Jordan, B. (1975), Is the Client a Fellow Citizen?, *Social Work Today,* 30 October.

Jordan, B. (1990), *Social Work in an Unjust Society,* Harvester Wheatsheaf.

Laming, H. (1989), Meet the Challenge, *Community Care,* 3 August.

Marsh, P. and Fisher, M. (1992), *Good Intentions: Developing partnership in the social services,* Joseph Rowntree Foundation.

Newburn, T. (1993), *Making a Difference? Social work after Hillsborough,* National Institute for Social Work.

Pollock, A. (1994/5), The Creeping Privatisation of Community Care, *Health Matters,* 20, Winter.

Public Health Alliance (1988), *Beyond Acheson: An agenda for the new public health,* PHA.

Rogers, A., Pilgrim, D. and Lacey, R. (1993), *Experiencing Psychiatry: Users' views of services,* Macmillan/MIND.

Royal Society of Arts (1994), *Tomorrow's Company: The role of business in a changing world,* RSA.

Seed, P. (1990), *Introducing Network Analysis in Social Work,* Jessica Kingsley.

Smale, G. (1988), *Community Social Work: A paradigm for change,* National Institute for Social Work.

Smale, G. and Tuson, G. (1993), *Empowerment, Assessment, Care Management and the Skilled Worker,* HMSO.

Stevenson, O. (1993), Address to the Annual Conference of the Association of Directors of Social Services, June.

Stevenson, O. and Parsloe, P. (1993), *Community Care and Empowerment,* Joseph Rowntree Foundation.

Trevillion, S. (1992), *Caring in the Community: A networking approach to community partnership,* Longman.

Whitaker, D. and Archer, J. (1989), *Research by Social Workers: Capitalising on experience,* CCETSW.

Wistow, G. (1995), Coming Apart at the Seams, *Health Services Journal,* 2 March.

Editors and Contributors

Bob Anderson taught Social Work at Keele University for 20 years, ending up as Tutor-in-Charge of the two year postgraduate Diploma course. A strong teaching interest in volunteers and voluntary organisations was supported by personal practice in a range of local charities. In 1989 he joined Age Concern England, setting up its new Contracts Unit to advise Age Concern organisations on their community care contracts, and has produced extensive written guidance for them upon the subject.

Peter Beresford is a Senior Lecturer in Social Policy at Brunel University College, joint co-ordinator of Open Services Project and a member of Survivors Speak Out. He has a longstanding involvement in issues of participation and empowerment as worker, researcher and service user. He has written widely on the subject and is co-author of *The Politics of Participation*, (Routledge, forthcoming).

Maria Duggan has a background in social work, social work management and education. Currently she works as an independent researcher, management consultant and trainer on community care and health and social policy. Maria has worked across the health and social care divide since 1984 and is particularly interested in the development of primary care. Most recently she has completed work for the Kings Fund Centre, the NHS Executive and Nuffield Institute for Health and the Institute of Public Policy Research.

Miriam Hastings has a PhD from the University of London, where she works as a part-time lecturer in cross-cultural literature. She runs supportive, creative groups for women survivors of mental distress, funded by Birkbeck College and held at the Mary Ward Centre in London. She also works as an independent consultant and trainer in mental health, and as freelance researcher and writer. Her contribution published here is drawn from work she wrote for a *Survivors' Guide to Training Approved Social Workers*, which she co-authored with David Crepaz-Keay, and which is now available from the Central Council for Education and Training in Social Work.

Julian Le Grand is the Richard Titmuss Professor of Health Policy at the London School of Economics and Professorial Fellow at the Kings Fund Policy Institute. He was previously Professor of Public Policy at the University of Bristol and a Lecturer in Economics at the London School of Economics and at the University of Sussex. He is the author of many articles and books on the welfare state, including most recently *Quasi-Markets and Social Policy* (with Will Bartlett, Macmillan, 1993) and *Evaluating the NHS Reforms* (with Ray Robinson, Kings Fund, 1994).

Denise Platt was appointed as Under Secretary, Social Services, at the Association of Metropolitan Authorities in November 1994. Previously Director of Social Services, London Borough of Hammersmith and Fulham, she began her career as a hospital social worker in 1968 after graduating in Economics at University College Cardiff, and has held a number of practitioner and senior managerial posts in social services in London. She is the Chair of the National AIDS Trust, a member of CCETSW Council, Chair of the National Institute for Social Work Research Consultative Committee, and a past President of the Association of Directors of Social Services.

Kath Gillespie Sells has a background in health and education. Following disablement in 1981, she was employed as a principal officer in a local authority funded disability organisation as head of training, and is currently working in the voluntary sector as a welfare rights adviser. She is also a freelance training consultant and researcher and writer in the area of equalities, and a volunteer counsellor at PACE, the counselling service for lesbians and gay men, offering a service to disabled people by a disabled counsellor.

Steve Trevillion is a Senior Lecturer in Social Work and Social Policy at Brunel University College. He has long-standing interests in both social work education and community care. He has been a social worker and practice teacher and for the last nine years has been working full-time in social work education. At present he is the course leader of a large Diploma in Social Work course whilst also being actively involved in developing a post-qualifying MSc course in Collaborative Community Care. Steve Trevillion is the author of *Caring in the Community: A* *networking approach to community partnership* (Longman, 1992) and co-author with Peter Beresford of *Developing Skills for Community Care: A collaborative approach* (Arena 1995).

Daphne Statham is Director of the National Institute for Social Work. She has 30 years experience in the fields of social services and education and training. The main focus of her practice has been on children and families. In training she began as a practice teacher and subsequently moved into college based teaching. Since 1971 she has worked with service user organisations as a volunteer, as joint contractor and on national forums. She has maintained contact with education, training and research through her external examinership of programmes and dissertations, undertaking work on the Review of the Diploma in Social Work, and membership of CCETSW Council from 1991 to 1994.

Sir William Utting held senior positions in the probation service, local government and central government. He was chief professional adviser on social services and social work to the Secretary of State from 1976 to 1991, when he retired from the Department of Health as Chief Inspector of Social Services. He is now Chairman of the National Institute for Social Work, Deputy Chair of the Council of Goldsmiths College, and a Trustee of the Rowntree Foundation, Community Service Volunteers and the Mental Health Foundation. He is a member of the Nolan Committee.

Jan Wallcraft, a former recipient of psychiatry, is currently a research scholar at South Bank University, studying user perspectives on alternatives to psychiatric hospital for people in crisis. She has been a member of the national self-advocacy organisation Survivors Speak Out for many years and was the first co-ordinator of MINDLINK, MIND's national user network. She has made a special study of ECT, women's issues in mental health, and holistic alternatives to medication. She is also a practitioner of aromatherapy, massage and reflexology. She has two children at college.